THE BUTTER COOKBOOK

Smith
Street
Books

THE BUTTER

A complete guide to
the ultimate ingredient

MONICA CAVARZAN

COOKBOOK

CONTENTS

The LONG LIFE *of* BUTTER

. . .

After working with it for more than 10 years, butter isn't just an ingredient for me – it's a story I continue telling. I've churned it, shaped it, wrapped it, handed it over the counter and watched people's faces when they taste it. I have cooked with it, baked with it and, of course, eaten it. It carries history, memory and a kind of quiet joy.

For a long time, butter was just there – a block in the fridge. Something you didn't think much about until you needed to grease a pan or finish a sauce. Then the world sped up, food became more industrialised and butter suddenly found itself labelled too rich, too fat, too naughty, too old-fashioned.

But those same shifts in food have pushed many of us back towards ingredients that are real. In a sea of numbers, additives and marketing claims, butter stands there with its short ingredient list and straight-up honesty: cream, maybe cultures, maybe salt, plus time, skill and a human being willing to show up, batch after batch.

As a butter-maker – and after meeting other butter-makers like myself – I see both the beauty and the cost. Cream isn't cheap. Small dairy farms are under pressure. Making butter properly takes time and attention, and there's no short-cut button you can press. That's why good butter costs more, but that's also exactly why it matters.

This book is my ode to butter. It's a celebration, but it's also my chance to explain why this ingredient deserves to be seen as so much more than something to spread on toast. If it's transformation you're after, just agitate some cream and watch what happens: the process itself is beautiful. Whether you're spreading butter thick, folding it through pastry, or just pausing to think about the farmers and makers behind it, I hope these pages bring you back to real food.

Butter isn't dying – we're just finally noticing it again.

Monica

Founder and butter-maker, Lard Ass Butter

THE STORY

OF BUTTER

BUTTER *through the* AGES

The history of butter has been spread too thin.

That's a butter joke. There are lots of them and, once you start, you can't stop.

The origins of butter are murky, yet intriguing. I read once that it was discovered by accident, like many iconic foods with staying power. Cornflakes come to mind, and wine, and popcorn. Butter is said to have been discovered around 3000–2000 BCE in the steppe regions of either Mesopotamia or Central Asia, where milk was transported in animal-skin bags by nomads who would do much walking or horseback riding. It was this agitation that was the cause of great surprise when the nomad opened his or her bag to discover beautiful yellow globules of delicious butter floating in the milk.

As a butter-maker, I have mental images of the nomad sitting at the base of a shady tree for a mid-morning rest, taking up the little buttons of butter from the animal-skin bag and slathering them on a crusty baguette. Alas, this did not happen! Butter in those early days was used more for medicinal purposes and was more likely to have been smeared like an ointment over a grazed knee or on a face prickling from too much sun. I am quietly confident, however, that the transition from medicine to foodstuff would not have required much persuasion.

So, it seems butter is least 4000 years old – possibly much older. The word 'butter' derives from the Ancient Greek words for cow and cheese, or 'bous' and 'turos' – still relevant today wherever butter is made from cow's milk.

During ancient Roman and early medieval times, butter was seen as a crude form of fat compared to olive oil, which was prized but more difficult to produce or import. The keeping quality of butter during those times led to its being considered a food for peasants. However, rancid butter was common, due to the lack of refrigeration, and butter spoilt particularly quickly in the Mediterranean climate, so it was generally made in the cooler parts of Europe. This led to a cultural divide that exists even today – olive oil in Europe's south versus butter in the north.

Historical myths might paint a picture of our Stone Age ancestors wandering about with clay cups of fresh milk in hand but, in truth, nothing could be further from reality. In Neolithic times, milk was too precious – and too perishable – to be consumed fresh. Fresh, unpasteurised milk sours in hours without refrigeration, especially in the warmth of the day. Most adults at the time were lactose intolerant, making fresh milk a recipe for stomach trouble.

Instead, our ancestors relied on the ingenuity of fermentation, turning milk into cheese and yoghurt and other cultured products that live on today. These include kefir from the Caucasus Mountains; ayran, the savoury yoghurt drink from Türkiye and Armenia; cooling fruit lassi, from India and Pakistan; qurut, the dried fermented milk balls from Central Asia, prepared in many countries and known by many names; and, of course, countless traditional fermented cheeses, such as paneer, labneh, halloumi and Icelandic skyr.

Fermentation is a process that allowed our ancestors to preserve food and extend its life well beyond the limits of freshness – and many of these cultured products are making a comeback today as we understand and appreciate more about their health benefits.

ABOVE Dairy products make from yak's milk in Mongolia

BUTTER FERMENTS *around the* WORLD

Fermented dairy is one of humanity's oldest and most diverse food traditions. These products all share the same underlying principle: they use beneficial microbes to transform fresh milk into something long-lasting, nutritionally enhanced and safer to eat. These different foods developed in response to local climates, religious or ritual purposes, milk sources and cultural tastes, each carrying the stamp of the communities they come from.

Cultured butter

Enjoyed around the world, cultured butter is made from cream that is fermented with lactic acid bacteria before churning. Before commercialisation, it was made by leaving a bucket of milk in the warmest part of the room, allowing the cream to rise to the top and encouraging the bacteria in the unpasteurised milk to do its magic. The cream was skimmed from the top of the bucket and churned into butter.

Fermented ghee

Ghee is made by slowing simmering butter to remove the water and milk solids, leaving a pure fat; fermented ghee is made by using cultured butter during this process. Ideal for hot climates, as it's very shelf stable in high temperatures, ghee originated in many regions, including South Asia, the Middle East and parts of Africa. It is sometimes aged for months or years to develop medicinal qualities (known in Ayurveda as 'old ghee' or 'purana ghee').

Yak butter

Found in China, Nepal, Bhutan and Mongolia, yak butter is made from yak milk, which is sometimes lightly fermented first for preservation. Butter is added to the famous Tibetan butter tea, po cha. In Nepal, the milk from chauri (a cross between a cow and a yak) is dried and fermented into the hard and chewy churpi, which provides concentrated fat and calories for those living a nomadic life in the mountains.

Suero de mantequilla

With a name meaning 'butter serum' or 'butter whey', this is a version of buttermilk. Made by communities living in Latin America, the buttermilk is captured from churning fermented cream and used as a sour, probiotic-rich drink or base for sauces.

Smen and semneh

Smen was developed in North Africa by salting butter in jars and leaving it to ferment until it took on a sharp, very cheesy pungency resembling rancid butter. It's a way of preserving butter for months, even years, and gives a deep umami flavour to savoury dishes.

Across the Red Sea in Yemen, semneh is prepared by slowly clarifying butter and flavouring it with spices such as fenugreek, cumin, turmeric and garlic. It can then be stored for months at room temperature and is used as a base for cooking. Like ghee, it is not always fermented, but can be.

Smen is prized for its tang and intensity, added sparingly at the end of cooking to flavour a dish. Semneh is savoury and aromatic, used generously as a cooking fat to infuse breads, stews and rice with spice and richness.

Fermented butters

During the Middle Ages, in countries such as Norway, Iceland and Ireland, butter was sometimes buried in bogs or packed into barrels with salt, allowing it to ferment and keep for long periods of time as a means of preserving fat during harsh winters. This process did more than just preserve though: it produced strong, distinctive flavours that were cherished in their own right. Today, these countries still produce fermented butters artisanally.

• • •

SYMBOLISM AND RITUAL

Butter's earliest life did not start at the dining table. Even once it had made the leap from ointment to edible, butter wasn't viewed as a food to be placed in bowls and eaten with bread, or melted in a pan to cook with as we know it today. It was used for its symbolic meaning before it was a food of pleasure. Butter and butter-like fats were considered substances set aside for ritual in various ancient civilisations. In today's modern world, some cultures continue to use butter and ghee in the same way – offered into flames, lit in lamps and moulded into special forms.

Other foods, of course, carry this double symbolism of feeding the body as well as the spirit. In Christianity, bread is no ordinary staple but the body of Christ itself, broken and shared as a sign of communion. And long before the Eucharist began, Egyptians placed loaves of bread in tombs, believing that the dead, like the living, would need nourishment for the journey ahead. Bread was food, but it was also continuity – the stuff of life.

Wine, too, crossed the line between sustenance and symbol. The ancient Greeks poured wine on the ground as libation, a gift to their gods, and in the Jewish and Christian traditions, it holds the place of ritual and joy; to drink wine is to participate in something greater than daily nourishment. It is to commune with divinity.

In the Bible, salt represents permanence and purity, and was often used to seal agreements or covenants. In Japan, salt continues to be scattered in Shinto rituals to purify spaces, warding off the touch of evil spirits. In South and East Asian cultures, rice is offered at temples, heaped into bowls as a gift to the gods, or scattered over newlyweds as a blessing of fertility and prosperity. As the grain of life, rice links daily sustenance with the cycles of birth and renewal.

So, it should be no surprise that butter and ghee have a similarly meaningful role in many cultures. In India, ghee is more than just an ingredient: it is an identity, woven into daily meals, ceremonies and sacred traditions, and therefore holds a place of extraordinary importance. For over 3000 years, it has been poured into sacred fires during Vedic ceremonies, each spoonful believed to carry prayers skyward. It flickers in temple lamps as a symbol of purity and light.

In Hindu mythology, Krishna's stories include his time as the butter thief Makhan Chor. He steals butter from pots hidden by village women, smears it on his companions and revels in its abundance. In these tales, butter is joy itself – a reminder that the divine can be mischievous as well as holy.

High in the Himalayas, yak butter serves a different spiritual purpose. In Tibetan Buddhist monasteries, butter lamps glow day and night, their steady flames thought to dispel both physical and spiritual darkness. Butter here is also transformed into art: monks use yak butter mixed with flour and pigments to mould elaborate butter sculptures, or torma, during festivals, knowing they will melt away. These sculptures, fragile and fleeting, embody the Buddhist truth of impermanence – beauty that vanishes as quickly as it appears.

In parts of East Africa, too, butter steps beyond sustenance. Fermented butter and ghee are used in anointing rituals, blessings and marriage ceremonies. Smoothed on skin and offered at unions, they carry meanings of purity, prosperity and continuity – symbols of life carried forward into new generations.

OPPOSITE CLOCKWISE FROM TOP A torma in a Tibetan monastery; A Buddhist rice offering; Ghee candles lit in India

BOG BUTTER

For ancient communities in the boglands of Ireland and Northern Europe, butter represented two elements of life – symbolism and survival. Archaeologists have uncovered great lumps of 'bog butter' buried deep under wet peat thousands of years ago, where the conditions are like a fridge. The cool and acidic environment with low oxygen helped keep the butter from spoiling for long periods of time, sometimes centuries.

So, why was butter buried? Just for preservation? Well, some say it was a gift to the gods of earth and fertility. Others see it as a store of wealth and nourishment hidden away from thieves, invading armies or even tax collectors. In medieval Ireland, butter was used to pay rent to landlords. It was so prized that it filled cellars and granaries alongside grain, forming part of the wealth that supported entire estates.

The act of burial, whether ritual or practical, gave butter a sacred charge: to feed not just the body, but the mysteries of life and death.

Bog butter deposits continue to be uncovered in farmlands throughout Ireland and Scotland, with a find in 2013 revealing a 47 kg (around 100 lb) bundle over 3000 years old. It's now on display at the National Museum of Ireland.

ABOVE Depiction of the Hindu diety Krishna demanding a butter tax

OPPOSITE The Butter Tower of Rouen's Cathedral

FROM FOOD TO CURRENCY

From bog butter to yak tea, butter became both sacred and practical across cultures: a substance that carried meaning while sustaining life. Yet, once households were able to secure enough for themselves, it seems butter's role transformed. With time, and with the arrival of technologies that made it possible to store and transport it more reliably, butter's fate as a commodity was sealed.

Butter began to circulate outwards, becoming something that shaped economies and built monuments. From the moment it could be stored, moved and measured, it stepped into a new role as a form of wealth to be bartered between households, taxed by rulers, and even used as a form of currency. Its journey from churn to market reflects not only the value placed on nourishment, but also the way food itself became a driver of economies.

In Scandinavia, butter became a staple of trade across the Viking world. It was stored in barrels and travelled on ships alongside other commodities like fish and furs, carried as a portable form of nourishment and wealth. For these seafaring societies, butter was both food and an export that tied distant communities together.

By the late Middle Ages in Europe, butter's status had grown even further. As Catholic fasting rules loosened, particularly in France and Germany, butter surged in demand as a replacement for meat and lard on religious fast days. Cathedrals were even built, in part, on butter money.

A wonderful example is Rouen Cathedral in France, which houses three towers, the tallest of which is Tour de Beurre – the Butter Tower. During Lent fasting, the consumption of butter was not allowed. However, Archbishop Robert de Croixmare obtained a Papal dispensation that allowed donors to the tower's construction to carry on eating their rich Normandy butter. Work began on the tower in 1485 with plenty of keen donors! Here, butter was literally transformed into stone – food turned into faith and faith into architecture.

In colonial times, butter was part of the trade triangle. Irish butter was shipped in large quantities to the Caribbean to feed enslaved people on plantations, a darker chapter that underscores how commodities often tie into systems of exploitation. At the same time, in North America, butter became a marker of self-sufficiency and was traded in local markets, with families measuring prosperity in part by how much butter they could sell or barter.

SALTED *or* UNSALTED?

When we buy butter at the supermarket today, for most of us there is only one choice that needs making: salted or unsalted? This is a choice that first started in France, and it's an interesting quirk of history as to why that country ended up with two very distinct butter traditions, which both still live on.

For centuries, the great divide came down to one simple thing: salt. Who had it, who could afford it, and who was forced to pay heavily for it.

Inland regions of France, particularly those around Paris and the central north regions, such as Burgundy, Champagne and parts of Normandy, faced steep salt taxes under the gabelle, a notoriously unfair French tax that was in place from the fourteenth century until its abolition in 1790. It made salt expensive and often inaccessible to many people. As a result, butter was eaten fresh and unsalted, because adding salt for preservation simply wasn't economical. This 'sweet' butter became the foundation of Parisian cuisine and is the reason why so many French pastries call for unsalted butter today.

But the story of butter plays out differently on the country's west coast, where the salty ocean laps the shores. Regions such as Brittany and Pays de la Loire were salt rich. They had abundant access to salt from marshes and, importantly, were mostly exempt from the salt tax. Salt was cheap, plentiful and part of daily life. So, butter there was traditionally salted, for both flavour and preservation. Salting the butter meant it lasted longer, travelled further and developed its own distinct character. The salted butters of Brittany, in particular, became famous for their depth, minerality and keeping quality.

So, the great French butter divide wasn't initially about taste – it was about economics, geography and taxation. Two cultures, two traditions, shaped by something as simple as the price of salt. Those historical divides laid the groundwork for the regional butter styles we recognise today, many of which are now protected under formal French and European classifications.

BUTTER COWS – AND A BUTTER ELVIS

Tibet's monks are not the only people who carve butter. In Renaissance Europe, sculptures made of butter were used for decorating banquet tables and lavish dining occasions by priests and politicians alike. Starting in the Middle Ages, Catholics in Eastern Europe began to form butter into the shape of a lamb for a small Easter table sculpture, hand-shaped or pressed into a mould. Still made today, these lambs stand for the Paschal Lamb, a reminder of Christ's sacrifice on Good Friday, with some families pressing a tiny butter cross on its back to 'mark' the symbol of goodness. Like the Tibetan tormas, the butter lamb is meant to be both seen and shared. It is blessed, admired and then eaten with the holiday meal.

In 1876, a butter bas-relief carving, created by Caroline Shawk Brooks and called *Dreaming Iolanthe,* was shown at Philadelphia's Centennial Exhibition, where it caused a sensation. To keep it intact during its display, it was suspended above a bucket of ice that had to be topped up constantly.

Like many farm women, Brooks churned the family's butter for both home use and to earn money. Instead of relying on the tin moulds that were common then to make hers stand out to customers, she hand-carved shells, animals and faces, often using improvised tools. The novelty and the likenesses drew attention. Commissions followed, including a much-talked-about portrait of Mary, Queen of Scots.

Norma 'Duffy' Lyon became Iowa's premier butter sculptor after 1999, when she made a rendition of *The Last Supper* out of butter. This brought her national attention, but she was also known in America as the 'Butter-Cow Lady' thanks to the tons of US Grade AA salted butter she sculpted into life-sized cows starting in 1959. Lyon was also known for carving popular celebrities, including Elvis Presley, Garth Brooks and Tiger Woods. In 2007, she came out of retirement briefly to carve a slightly wonky bust of Barack Obama.

State fairs across America still gear up for butter sculpting exhibitions every year. By August, the height of the state fair season, many tons of butter will have been layered over frames of wire and canvas to form artworks such as the Empire State Building, full-size cars, celebrities and, of course, the ever-popular butter cow. The Iowa State Fair has showcased its iconic life-sized butter cow for more than a century, and the Utah, Ohio and Illinois state fairs also treat it as a staple attraction. The spectacle blends craft and dairy education – visitors watch artisans working at refrigerator temperatures, learn about milk, cream and butterfat, and marvel at ephemeral works.

RIGHT *Dreaming Iolante* by Caroline Shawk Brooks

THE FRIDGE CHANGES EVERYTHING

Today, butter is a commodity traded on global markets, its price influenced by weather, politics and supply chains. Countries such as Ireland, New Zealand and the Netherlands reign as the world's leading butter exporters and account for well over half of the world's total exports. In 2024, New Zealand led the world with approximately 18.4 per cent of the export market, thanks to global dairy cooperative and processor Fonterra who controls 30 per cent of global dairy exports. Ireland was just behind at 17 per cent, while the Netherlands sent out 13.8 per cent.

Collectively, that's a lot of butter being shipped around the globe and, as consumers, we get to enjoy butter from the other side of the world appearing in our local supermarkets. Brands such as Kerry Gold, Lurpak, Mainland, President, Anchor and, to a lesser degree, smaller French 'boutique' brands like Beurre d'Isigny and Beurre d'Échiré, are available thanks to the technology of refrigeration. That single invention revolutionised butter from perishable to profitable, thanks to refrigeration pioneer Mr James Harrison in the 1850s. And he just happened to be situated in Geelong, Australia.

What began in Geelong with Harrison's refrigeration success turned into the Victorian Ice Works, and it not only changed international trade but also shaped Australia's own relationship with butter. From the earliest of days of colonial settlement, dairy farming had been both a livelihood and a challenge, with butter at its heart. As settlers adapted European traditions to Australian soil, climate and conditions, they laid the foundations for a butter industry that would grow into one of our country's defining food stories.

ABOVE The original ice-making machine in 1862, patented by James Harrison in 1859

BUTTER IN AUSTRALIA

Australia's dairy production story didn't follow the same artisan-to-industrial arc as Europe's. Instead, it was shaped by immigrants who brought with them influences from an industrialised world – namely, convicts.

Australia was colonised in 1788, at the very moment the Industrial Revolution was reshaping Britain. The convicts and soldiers were sent with the necessities and comforts believed essential to establish a colony: a small herd of cattle, a handful of sheep, goats and pigs, along with wooden churns, farm tools and the knowledge of European dairying.

From the outset, dairying was framed less as a craft and more as a utilitarian pursuit – focused first on survival, then productivity and, eventually, the possibility of export. Convicts were assigned to the heavy labour of milking cows and churning cream into butter, while officers and settlers oversaw the herds and guarded the colony's precious livestock.

Historically, it was the women who made butter, while the men tended to the fieldwork and other heavy, outdoor labour – 'man with plough, woman with cow.' The term 'milk maid' was coined simply because, from Europe to North America to Australia, women were traditionally the ones who milked the cows, skimmed the cream and churned the butter – often by hand and often daily.

Butter was not plentiful during Australia's early years of colonisation. The heat made fresh milk spoil quickly, while churns produced only small amounts at a time. Yet, even so, it became part of the colony's ration system, with convicts sometimes issued small allowances alongside flour, salted meat and grain. In this way, butter occupied a unique position in colonial life: simultaneously a rare comfort and a symbol of survival, its production grounded in convict labour and its traditions transplanted from Europe.

Europe had had centuries to develop regional, artisan dairy traditions, such as English farmhouse Cheddar. Early butter production in Australia focused more on shelf life and exportability, and less on regional flavours – unsurprising, considering the cows weren't local breeds. They had also been sent across from Europe.

Skipping the centuries-long agrarian peasant farmer evolution, Australia, instead, adopted British dairy models from the start, building systems quickly to supply colonies, goldfields and, later, British export markets. From this they moved swiftly to co-operative butter factories; the first started up in 1888 in Cobden, Victoria, where it is still in operation today.

Factory churns quickly replaced hand-churn methods by the late 1800s to increase production and volume for shipment as Australia's population grew. The manufacturing guidelines were essentially focused on meeting British grading standards, rather than creating local taste or terroir.

By the late nineteenth century, butter in Australia had moved well beyond the household churn. Small communities pooled their resources across dairying districts, establishing butter factories that were practical and steam driven. Farmers brought in their cream daily for churning and packing and, in return, they received a steady income as their butter was processed and sent off to city grocers or export markets.

The early twentieth century brought another surge in dairying, with the Soldier Settlement schemes after World War I and again after World War II. Returning servicemen were granted small parcels of land, many of which were turned into dairy farms, dramatically expanding Australia's

ABOVE Cream being checked at a Queensland butter factory in 1932
OPPOSITE CLOCKWISE FROM TOP Victoria's Mirboo North Butter Factory in 1912; Inside an Australian butter factory between 1921 and 1924; Men gathered at the Great South Co-operative Butter Factory in Foster, Victoria, in 1929

dairying footprint. Butter factories became essential outlets for these new farmers and, at their peak, there were dozens of butter factories scattered across Victoria, New South Wales and Queensland, each one a hub of both economic activity and community life that bound people together. They stood as symbols of cooperation and were often named Co-ops or Cooperations, where farmers worked together to ensure their produce met the growing demand for Australian butter.

The factories themselves were sturdy and functional, often built of brick or timber with cool rooms and tall chimneys that signalled the presence of steam engines inside. They hummed with the rhythmic churn of butter, the hiss of steam and the comings and goings of horse-drawn carts, followed later by trucks.

By the early twentieth century, Australia's butter industry was at its peak. In 1908 there were 560 butter factories operating across the country, with 579 by 1920. These were not small-scale sheds; they were the beating heart of rural communities, supplied by hundreds of modest dairy farms averaging 15–30 cows each. Farmers would cart their cream daily to the local factory, where it was churned, salted and packed for both domestic and export markets.

Korumburra in Gippsland, Victoria, was home to a butter factory established in 1895. At its peak, it was considered the largest butter factory in the Southern Hemisphere, a testament to the scale and ambition of Australia's early dairy industry. (The factory closed in 1972, marking the end of an era, though the site later found new life in the early 1990s when Burra Foods commenced dairy processing operations in the same building.)

Victoria had 175 factories still operating by 1937, while New South Wales followed closely with 130. All stood as symbols of local community and pride. Butter, once a household chore of churning, had transformed into a massive national industry, bolstered by refrigeration and shipping that carried Australian butter to the breakfast tables of Britain.

MIRBOO
NORTH
BUTTER FACTORY

REGISTERED
OFFICE
GREAT SOUTHERN
CO-OPERATIVE Co.Y LTD

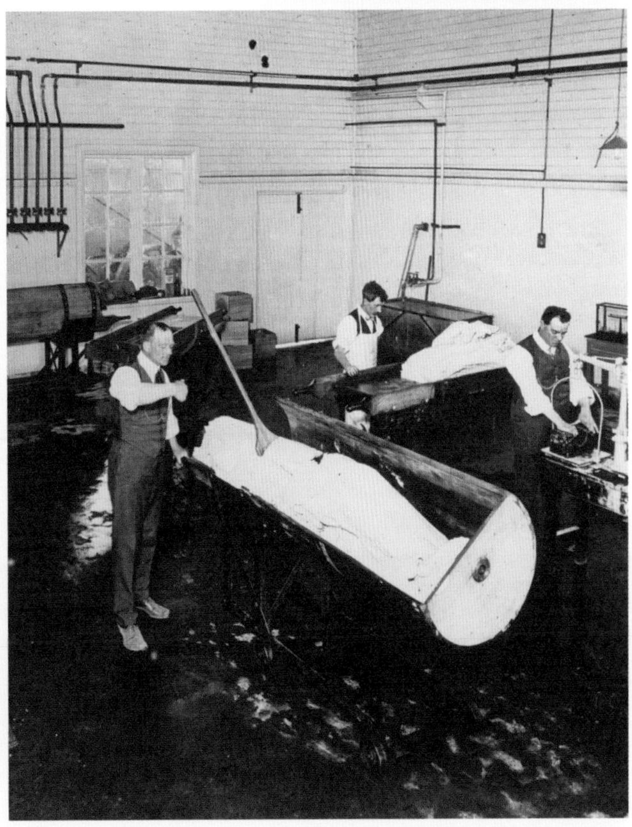

• • •

AND THE FALL OF THE BUTTER FACTORIES

Yet this golden era was not to last. By the mid-twentieth century small butter factories began to close, replaced by larger, centralised plants and, eventually, multinational processors.

Today, these buildings no longer serve their original purpose. The age of the local butter factory has long since passed. Yet the old factories remain, some repurposed into homes, art galleries or community halls. Many are protected by the National Trust, recognised for their role in shaping rural life and standing as quiet witnesses to a time when butter was not just food, but a cornerstone of Australia's rural economy and identity.

Victoria's Glenormiston Butter and Cheese Factory, also known as the Noorat Butter Factory, began churning butter in a repurposed woolshed in 1895. The striking red-brick factory was built in 1924 near the farming town of Noorat. Over 100 years later, the building is part of a project to provide a range of accommodation for key agricultural workers and their families.

In New South Wales, the Bega Co-operative Creamery was founded in 1899. It grew out of the butter factory model and became the Bega Cheese Company we know today – a modern dairy giant. Moss Vale Butter Factory was also built in the 1890s and tells part of the Southern Highlands' dairying story. While it no longer makes butter, the building remains a local landmark.

In Queensland, Maleny dairy farmers opened their own butter factory in 1904 to avoid the long trek to Brisbane, with the first cream processed at Maleny Butter Factory in December that year. These days, the well-preserved building is the town's arts and community centre.

The Mersey Vale Butter and Cheese Factory was founded in northern Tasmania in 1893, and later evolved into the Mersey Valley brand we find in our stores now. Their cheese products carry the heritage of that original co-operative, linking Tasmania's dairying past to its modern identity.

The Duck River Butter Factory that opened in 1904 became one of Tasmania's most famous butter brands, synonymous with quality. The factory was also a cornerstone of the region's co-operative movement, helping small farmers thrive.

In the late 1800s and early 1900s, small cooperative butter factories – such as Laura Butter Factory and Mount Gambier Butter Factory – also popped up across dairying districts of South Australia, reflecting the rapid growth of dairying in the rich volcanic soils of the South East. Many were later absorbed into larger co-operatives, or shut down when centralised processing took over in the mid-twentieth century.

Western Australia's Busselton Butter Factory was built in 1918, when dairying in the South West was expanding, and operated until 1952. The building still stands, transformed into the Busselton Museum, preserving the district's dairying and agricultural history.

Canberra's oldest dairy building, Duntroon Dairy, was built in 1832 by Robert Campbell, the Scottish merchant known as the Father of Australian Commerce. Duntroon Dairy is the oldest surviving building in the ACT and one of the region's first butter-making sites. Its stone walls and in-ground cistern kept milk cool long before refrigeration, allowing tenant farmers to churn butter and produce cheese for local markets. Today, preserved by the National Trust, it offers a rare glimpse into Canberra's modest dairying beginnings.

Even in their stillness, these structures speak – monuments to an age when butter truly was Australia's golden commodity.

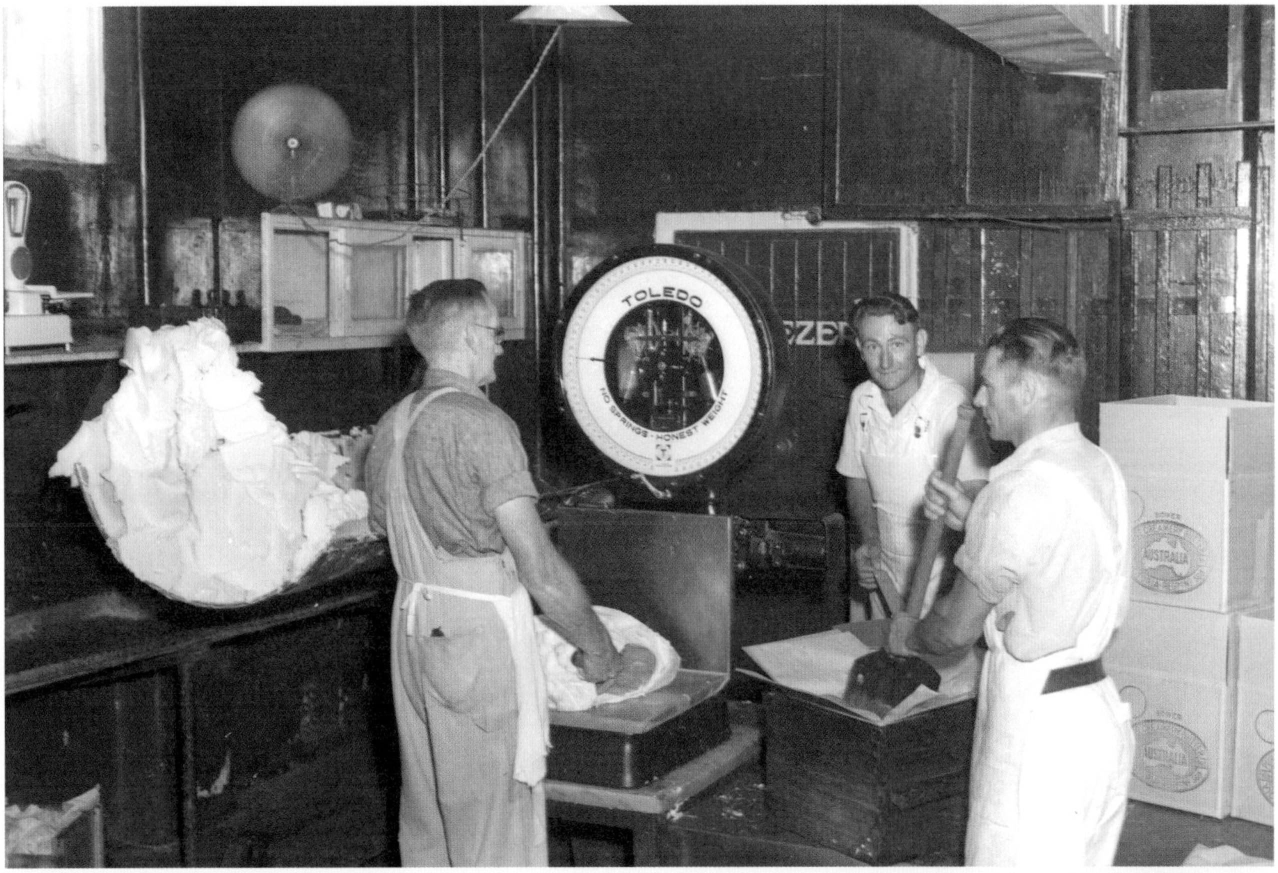

TOP TO BOTTOM Workers at Victoria's Gunbower Butter Factory in 1951 weighing and boxing butter; New South Wales' Hexam Butter Factory in the 1940s

The MARGARINE WARS: *the* CALL *for* *a* SUBSTITUTE

It was in 1869 that the French government sought out a substitute for butter. A reward was offered to anyone who could create a cheap, stable butter alternative to feed both the army and the poorer classes. Butter's rise in cultural status had made it less accessible to ordinary people, and its production was still tied to the limits of the seasons.

This rise in butter's cultural status had taken place around 100 years earlier when the art of butter-making became a royal pastime in France. Marie Antoinette, Queen of France, famously had a rustic retreat built at the Palace of Versailles called the Hameau de la Reine ('The Queen's Hamlet'). It had a working dairy, complete with cows, goats and a milking parlour, with a laiterie (dairy room) where fresh milk, cream and butter were served in fine Sévres porcelain, like a butter tea party. Suddenly, butter was elegant, pastoral and aristocratic.

Before Marie Antoinette, butter in France had been seen largely as a regional, rustic food. But through the Queen's sudden interest in freshly churned butter, what was once a staple of northern farm kitchens was repositioned as something refined and fashionable for the elite. The Queen, of course, also had quite a penchant for cake – and met her fate with the guillotine in 1793.

Suet, stomach and a bit of udder

In response to the government's request for a butter substitue, French chemist Hippolyte Mège-Mouriès responded by submitting something he already been working on. He won, which is perhaps no surprise, for his was the only entry!

The inventor noticed that cows kept producing fat in their milk, even when they were undernourished. He guessed the fat must come from the cow's own body. To mimic this, he chopped up beef suet, mixed in animal stomach and simmered it in slightly alkaline water. The result looked like butter, but the taste wasn't right. Believing it needed 'more cow', he added chopped udder. This odd experiment became margarine.

He called it oleomargarine – 'oleum' for fat and 'margarite' for pearl, on account of its pearlescent shine. Patented in 1871 and mass-produced by the 1880s, its only real advantage was price – it was cheaper than butter. Although neither the French army nor the poor seemed too keen on the new alternative.

Mège-Mouriès sold his patent to Dutch butter company Jurgens, which would later become part of Unilever. His invention marked the birth of margarine, the first major competitor to butter, especially during times of scarcity and war.

A tax on your spread!

By the late 1890s margarine was spreading across several continents. Passionate lobbying from dairy farmers in the United States led to the instalment of the federal Margarine Act, slapping a tax on margarine and demanding that its manufacturers pay prohibitive licensing fees. Some states placed an outright ban on margarine sales. Margarine had become polarising, not just in the home but politically, too. A Wisconsin senator famously stated that butter should come from the dairy, not the slaughterhouse. 'I want butter that has the natural aroma of life

and health. I decline to accept as a substitute caul fat, matured under the chill of death, blended with vegetable oils and flavoured by chemical tricks.' His quote sends chills, as it is so relevant today.

Newspaper cartoonists had a field day, sketching factories tossing everything from stray cats to soap, paint, arsenic and even old rubber boots into the vat to make margarine. At the same time a flood of questionable 'scientific' reports warned that the consumption of margarine might cause cancer or lead to insanity.

Pink margarine

By the early 1900s, colouring margarine pink was mooted as a way to distinguish it from the 'real thing.' While butter is naturally yellow, thanks to milk's betacarotene from cows feeding on fresh grass, margarine was made in industrial vats and presented as a sickly shade of grey. Margarine manufacturers were keen to colour this paste yellow, so that it would appeal more to the public. Butter producers were immediately up in arms, claiming yellow margarine was the last straw and an act of fraud and a deliberate ploy to trick the public. With this, pink margarine was imposed by 32 states in America – only to have the law overturned by the Supreme Court on the grounds that it was illegal to enforce food adulteration.

The healthy alternative?

By the mid-twentieth century, margarine production shifted from beef tallow to vegetable and seed oils like soybean, sunflower and canola. This change made it cheaper and helped position the spread as a modern product – lighter, more adaptable and marketed as healthier than butter. Because it was lower in saturated fats and free from animal fats, margarine was promoted as the answer to rising heart attacks in the Western world. The media eagerly got behind the movement, hailing margarine as a way to lower cholesterol and protect heart health.

Food companies seized on this opportunity, launching campaigns that painted butter as old-fashioned and even dangerous, while margarine became the slick, scientific alternative. Doctors endorsed it, governments recommended it and families bought into the promise that margarine was the responsible choice. For decades, butter's reputation suffered.

It wasn't until much later, when research revealed the dangers of trans fats in hydrogenated margarines, that the pendulum began to swing back. Butter, with its deep roots in tradition and natural simplicity, was ready to reclaim its place – no longer the villain, but once again a food of culture, craft and pure flavour.

ABOVE A 1952 American Dairy Association advertisement
RIGHT A 1948 advertisement from the National Association of Margarine Manufacturers

UNDERSTANDING

BUTTER

enAid
ltra Power

The SCIENCE *of* BUTTER

Good butter begins with good milk, which then becomes good cream. The cow produces milk after calving, and both the quantity and composition of that milk can shift over the months that follow. Where the cow lives, what she eats and the season she's milked in all influence the composition of her milk.

In the early days of butter-making, milk was poured straight from the cow into large, wide shallow pans and left to rest for hours, if not overnight, often in a cool dairy room with stone floors. The cream would rise slowly to the top, forming a rich golden layer that could be separated off. This was the most precious part – it would be carefully skimmed by hand, using a ladle, and collected ready for churning. Time consuming but rewarding.

Today, cream separation is faster, but equally important to the process of butter-making, thanks to the use of a centrifugal separator. Imagine a giant salad spinner… the milk is poured in and the spinner rotates at a very high speed. Because cream is lighter than skim milk, it naturally moves to the centre, while the heavier skim milk moves outwards. The machine directs them into separate streams – cream out of one spout, skim milk through another.

The cream is then pasteurised. Pasteurisation is the process whereby milk or cream is heated to destroy harmful microbes and deactivate enzymes that could spoil its flavour. The heat treatment is done at a higher temperature for cream than it is for milk or cheese-making: either 30 minutes at 74°C (165°F) or 15 seconds at 85°C (185°F). Cream needs this extra heat because it contains more solids.

From there, we can culture the cream by adding lactic bacteria and leaving it to ferment, if we are making cultured butter. Next comes tempering, where the cream is gently heated (it was cooled after pasteurising) and rested to condition the fat. This improves the texture and helps reduce fat loss once churning begins. Finally, the cream is ready for churning, working, packing and chilling, transforming liquid cream into a solid pat of butter.

. . .

TASTE AND TERROIR

Milk, just like wine, reflects its terroir. The unique combination of soil, pasture, climate, water quality and farming practices all affect the production. Milk from cows grazing on spring pasture is very different from milk collected in the dry heat of summer, and different again if the cows are feeding indoors in the cold of winter.

What goes in *does* affect what comes out when it comes to milk and cows, or any ruminant animal for that matter. The flavour of butter begins long before the cream reaches the churn. What a cow eats profoundly influences the composition of her milk — and therefore the taste, texture and even colour of butter.

On the farm where I grew up, grass wasn't available all year round due to scorching summers, but it was lush in spring. We also had paddocks of forage rape, which the cows loved. This crop is a natural way to encourage milk production, as it offers cows high-protein, high-energy fodder during the late autumn–winter, when pasture slows down. With its beautiful, bright flowers, it was a beacon to our cows, and there were instances when our family would have to scramble because the herd had broken through the fence to get free rein of their favourite snack!

A diet of silage (fermented pasture) or grain, doesn't just fill the cow's belly – it shapes her whole physiology, from her digestion to her metabolism, and ultimately the milk she makes. Fresh spring pasture with a variety of grasses and weeds is rich in betacarotene and unsaturated fats, which not only deepen the colour of butter but also influence its flavour and texture.

When her diet changes with the seasons, the fat and protein profile of the cow's milk changes, giving each batch of butter a slightly different character. (Our family herd once took the opportunity to enjoy an afternoon in a turnip paddock – the next morning's milk had a strong cruciferous odour and the flavour of boiled cabbage water!)

The colour of butter is a good indicator of the feed. White, pale butter often means the cows have been eating dry hay, silage or grain rather than fresh pasture. When cows graze on lush green grass, their milk is rich in chlorophyll and betacarotene, which gives cream and butter a natural golden hue. This seasonal colour shift is one of the clearest signs of how closely butter reflects the land and a cow's diet. To meet consumer expectations for a rich golden colour, some commercial producers add yellow colouring, which creates the appearance that their cows have been eating grass, even when this isn't the case.

For artisan butter-makers, the color of every batch is a reminder that all butter tells a story about the herd it came from.

BREEDS *of* COW

Jersey

Small in stature, quiet in demeanour and typically light cream to dark brown in colour with brown eyes, this cow originated on the English Channel Island of Jersey. Their milk contains high levels of butterfat and protein, although their overall yield is moderate.

Guernsey

This cow takes its name from another Channel Island. She is fawn or red and white in colour, and her persona is hardy and quiet. Her milk is rich in flavour, high in butterfat and protein, and has a golden-yellow tinge due to its high betacarotene content when she's fed on a fresh grass diet.

Holstein Friesian

These cows have been around for over 2000 years. Their name comes from two regions in northern Europe – Friesland in the Netherlands and Schleswig-Holstein in Germany. They're a big, hardy breed known for producing lots of milk, although it's not as rich in butterfat as milk from Jersey and Guernsey cows. With their classic black-and-white markings, Holstein Friesian are the most common dairy cows in Australia, making up more than 60 per cent of the country's milking herd.

Montbéliarde

Hailing from the Jura region in eastern France and known for producing milk that's perfect for making rich, creamy butter and cheese, these cows have a striking red-and-white coat and a calm, easy-going nature. Their milk is naturally high in butterfat and protein, which makes it a favourite for cheese-making.

Swiss Brown

One of the oldest dairy breeds in the world, these are the grand dames of dairy, with records tracing their history over 4000 years in the Swiss Alps. While the protein-to-fat ratio to in their milk makes it especially prized for cheese- and butter-making, Swiss Browns are also loved by farmers for their docile and gentle personalities. My brother Louie has one in his dairy herd – Camilla – and it's his belief she responds to her name when called. Who am I to dispute cow behaviour?

Illawarra and Aussie Red

Originating from cross-breeding a number of varieties in the Illawarra region of New South Wales in Australia, these cows wear a beautifully rich red coat, some with specks of white. They are considered a hardy breed with medium to high milk yields. Their milk has a protein content, with a medium level of fat.

Ayrshire

Originally from Scotland, the Ayrshire breed is all about hardiness, agility and ability to thrive in tough conditions. Beautiful, with good temperament and butterfat, this cow is an efficient grazer and a gentle social herdmate.

Devon

Known for their deep, glossy red coats, these are often called Red Rubies. The Devon cow is one of the oldest and purest British cattle breeds. Though more commonly seen as a beef breed, their buttery legacy lives on in English farmhouse dairies.

BUTTER THROUGH THE SEASONS

Spring and early summer milk has a bold and beautiful golden colour due to the abundance and variety of fresh grass on the ground – it is often met with a warm welcome in the factory after the winter churning. With slightly lower total fat and higher unsaturated fatty acids, the butter is softer, more spreadable and has a deep golden-yellow colour and grassy flavour notes.

Late summer and early autumn milk often has a slightly higher fat content as the cows start eating more mature pasture and some supplemental feed, which helps boost milk solids. The milk's unsaturated fats carry more of a grassy, herbal compound, which gives summer butter its distinctive bright flavour. The colour is still golden and the flavour is more rounded with a silky mouthfeel.

Autumn is often a favourite season for butter-makers, because the balance of fat and protein creates excellent texture and complex flavours, especially when fermenting cream. The butter has a rich, firm texture, balancing spreadability with rounded flavour.

In winter, when the cows are feeding on silage, hay and grains (often indoors), the milk has higher saturated fats and lower carotene. The resulting butter is firmer, paler and less spreadable, with a cleaner slice and a milder flavour.

GRASS OR GRAIN?

Grass-fed cows, who have a diet of clover, ryegrass, lucerne and seasonal forage, such as turnip tops, produce milk that is higher in beneficial fatty acids, including omega-3s and conjugated linoleic acid (CLA). As their milk is rich in betacarotene, it has a deep golden-yellow hue, and its flavour can be described as 'grassy', 'herbal' or 'complex', reflecting terroir. Grass-fed butter is often firmer, more aromatic and varies with the seasons as pastures change.

Grain-fed cows, with a diet of mixed grains (corn, barley, wheat, sorghum), soy meal, and silage (common in feedlot or intensive systems), produce milk with a more consistent composition year-round. The milk is higher in omega-6 fatty acids, often has higher butterfat yields, and is pale cream or white in colour as less betacarotene is present. Grain-fed butter tends to be softer and more uniform in appearance. The flavour is milder than grass-fed.

Today, many large dairies use a mixed system – cows graze on pasture but are also supplemented with grain at milking time to balance energy intake. This approach smooths out seasonal fluctuations while maintaining grass-fed characteristics.

For the butter-maker, the difference isn't only nutritional – it's cultural and sensory. Grass-fed butter tells the story of a place, tasting of its soil, pasture and climate. It also has advantages in consistency and industrial reliability. Both have a role in the marketplace but, for the artisan, grass-fed cream is often prized for its complexity and authenticity.

CREAM IN BUTTER OUT

Cream is the layer of rich milk fat that naturally rises to the top of cow's milk when it's left to stand. In other milks – such as goat, sheep and buffalo – the fat stays more evenly dispersed, so the cream is harder to separate. This is one of the reasons cow's milk has became so widely used for cream and butter-making.

Not all butters are created equal. Butter is not a static, factory-produced slab of fat. It's a living product that carries the story of cow, cream and craft. What this means is that not all butters behave the same way.

At first glance, butter seems pretty basic – cream in, butter out, maybe some salt. To ensure butter stays butter, Americans went as far as writing a law in 1923 to define what butter should be: butter must come only from milk or cream, or both, with or without salt or added colouring, and contain at least 80 per cent milk fat by weight.

From a scientific point of view, butter is usually 80–82 per cent fat, 16–17 per cent water, 1.5 per cent salt, and around 1 per cent milk solids, such as vitamins, minerals and lactose.

So, yes, butter is simple – but it's the transformations that occur on the way from cream to butter that are surprisingly complex.

Quality of cream is equal to the quality of butter: it's that simple. Some important factors are considered when it comes to measuring quality, including milk fat content and pH. For making good butter, the milk fat should sit comfortably in the 36–42 per cent range. Below that, the yield efficiency drops; above that, the churn won't behave as it should and the butter can feel too rich, even oily.

The cream's pH also tells us a lot: pH is simply a measure of how acidic or alkaline something is, on a scale of 0 to 14. Water sits in the middle at pH 7 – perfectly neutral. Numbers below 7 mean more acidic (think lemon juice), while numbers above 7 mean more alkaline (like baking soda). Fresh cream should fall between 6.4 and 6.7; a lower number suggests unwanted bacterial activity.

Fat content and pH aren't the only counts that give a picture of overall microbial health, though. Dairy farmers have their milk tested at every batch to ensure all microbial factors are standard prior to sending anything to processing.

• • •

THE IMPORTANCE OF CREAM

Cream is a living, breathing food that continues to change and age, even after pasteurisation, just like milk. Each type has its own personality, but when it comes to sourcing cream for butter-making, you need one with the right fat content, a fresh flavour and no additives that interfere with the churn and final product. Once milk and cream are separated, there's a whole spectrum of cream types.

Single cream / light cream / reduced-fat cream
Around 18–20 per cent butterfat. Pourable and great for topping desserts, but too low in fat to whip into butter.

Pure cream / pouring cream
Usually 35 per cent milk fat but not necessarily formulated to whip well. This is meant to be poured over desserts or used in cooking where you want creaminess but not stiffness. So it's not ideal for butter-making – you would be whipping for a long time.

Whipping cream
Generally, contains around 36–40 per cent milk fat and is designed to whip into soft or firm peaks. Its higher fat content allows it to hold air and create a light, fluffy texture when whipped. Some companies add a thickener to this type of cream to help it whip. Check the packaging carefully and only buy brands of pure cream without any thickening agents added.

Thickened cream
Thickened cream has added thickeners (gelatin or carrageenan) to keep it stable. This is never good for butter-making as the thickener affects churning and texture.

Double / heavy cream
Around 48 per cent butterfat, this is very rich, almost spoonable and used for indulgent desserts or cooking. Could be made into butter but the mouthfeel would be too rich, almost fatty.

Clotted cream
Slowly heated and cooled cream with at least 55 per cent butterfat, producing a thick, yellow crust. Traditionally eaten with scones. Technically, could be churned into a dense butter although not at all cost effective and a waste of clotted cream!

Cultured cream
This is an umbrella term for any cream that has been started with live bacterial cultures and allowed to ferment (see the recipe for cultured butter on page 68). Both sour cream and crème fraîche fall into this category.

Sour cream
This is a fermented cream but with a fat content around 18–20 per cent, though sour cream made in small batches may be higher. Mildly tangy, creamy and very thick. Commercial sour cream is great for baked potatoes, soups, dips and salad dressings but not for butter-making.

Crème fraîche
Also a fermented cream but richer, with a higher fat content around 38–40 per cent. Crème fraîche is more stable for cooking than sour cream – perfect for stirring into hot dishes as it won't split. You shouldn't use commercial crème fraîche in butter-making, but you can use homemade versions to make cultured butter.

. . .

BUTTER'S STRUCTURE

The fat in milk is a mix of about 70 per cent saturated fat and 30 per cent unsaturated fat. Saturated fats (think lard) are solid at room temperature, while unsaturated fats are more liquid (think olive oil). This balance of fats is important, influencing butter's softness and melting point.

Because most of the fat in butter is in the form of triglycerides (little three-armed molecules of fatty acids that like to pack together neatly), this helps butter to stay solid. But while the ratio of fatty acids in milk is fairly consistent, small shifts are common. When a triglyceride suffers a change or weakens its links, the molecules don't stack as well. The structure becomes looser and butter softens or melts more easily.

You might have noticed the growth of 'spreadable' butter. In these products, the natural balance of fats is disrupted by introducting unsaturated fats – often seed oils – to make the butter more liquid at room temperature.

Fat composition can also be changed by another force – the cow. Cows being animals and not mechanised equipment, their milk isn't always the same. Fat, protein and mineral contents vary and while modern manufacturing processes are good at standardising the overall fat content, they can't correct inconsistencies in types of fats and their amounts: differences usually due to season, feed, lactation cycles, geography and the cow's breed.

These differences in fat ratios effect how milk behaves during butter-making, especially during emulsification (the blending of butter and water) which, in turn, influences butter's melting qualities and spreadability.

Butter also changes with age. Fresh butter is often softer, while older butter tends to firm up. This happens because some fats that were slow to crystallise eventually solidify, making butter harden: a reminder that butter always keeps evolving, even after it's been churned.

Fat doesn't just dictate butter's structure, though: it can also be the reason things go wrong during production.

Fat can spoil in two main ways. The first is the butter-maker's enemy, rancidity, which happens because of lipases.

Lipases are enzymes (a type of protein) that help calves digest fat by breaking down milk's triglycerides into free fatty acids and glycerol. (Humans have lipases for the same function.) Trouble during butter-making starts when the membranes of the liapses are damaged, either through rough handling of cream, poor storage, microbial contamination, or lapses during pasteurisation. Once lipases are loose, they snip apart triglycerides, releasing their free fatty acids. Some, including butyric acid, carry sour or soapy flavours.

That's why monitoring cream quality is critical: it helps keep those enzymes in check. It's worth noting that, when it comes to raw milk, lipases are very active – pasteurisation deactivates them.

But lipases are only half the story of butter production going bad.

Milk's triglycerides are packaged inside milk fat globules – tiny spheres of protection that guard quality. If those globules are damaged, the fat becomes vulnerable – not only to the liapses, snipping away, but to fat's second enemy: oxidation. When fat reacts with oxygen, it creates cardboard-like flavours: not what you want from your butter!

So, when it comes to making butter, it really comes down to fat: its ratio, quality and care. If you make your own butter at home, remember to handle your cream gently.

GHEE
(and clarified butter)

Ghee is one of the oldest and most revered forms of butter in the world. Made of just pure golden butterfat, it has a deep, toasty, nutty aroma.

Because it doesn't spoil easily, ghee has been used for centuries in hot climates. It's a staple in Indian and Pakistani kitchens, where it forms the base for curries, breads and sweets.

Within the ancient practice of Ayurveda, a belief system surrounding health and healing, ghee has been celebrated for thousands of years as both food and medicine. It is considered sattvic – meaning it's pure, balanced and known for giving nourishment to the body and calming the mind.

To make ghee, butter is slowly simmered until the water evaporates and the milk solids separate and brown slightly at the bottom of the pan. It's then strained to remove those milk solids (these are what can cause ghee to spoil or reduce its shelf life).

What remains is a clear, golden fat (also known as 'oil of milk') with a grainy texture. It is shelf stable, and has intensely aromatic hints of caramel and butterscotch. The process concentrates butter's richness while also eliminating lactose and casein, which means ghee keeps for longer and is suitable for those who are sensitive to dairy proteins.

With just the fat and no milk solids, ghee has a wonderfully high smoke point, making it ideal for frying and roasting when regular butter might burn. It's very shelf stable and can be stored in a pantry without refrigeration. But do keep it out of strong light and heat, store it in a glass jar (not plastic) and ensure the lid is tightly closed after each use.

With its high burning point, ghee can enhance flavour without burning foods like steaks, seafood and vegetables. The clarifying process means ghee can be also used for baking – it doesn't overpower subtle flavours.

Take care with measurements when using ghee as a straight substitute for butter, however. Ghee is 100 per cent fat, while butter is around 80 per cent fat and 17 per cent water, plus milk solids. The extra richness means you'll need a little less ghee than butter, and sometimes a splash of liquid to make up the difference. A good rule of thumb when swapping butter for ghee is to use 25 per cent less ghee.

Ghee is not the same things as clarified butter. This comes down to the process, which is important if you have a lactose or casein intolerance.

Clarified butter is made by simply melting butter until all the solids sit at the bottom of the pan, then straining off the solids and keeping the fat. Ghee is also made by separating butter's fat and solids, but cooking continues after this separation at a rolling boil until there is a nutty aroma and the solids turn golden brown. This cooks out the butter's moisture, which means ghee has a much longer shelf life than clarified butter. It also cooks out the lactose and casein, which clarified butter can still contain traces of.

Ghee can also be made with fermented cream, which brings a subtle tangy depth, similar to cultured butter. Buffalo milk ghee is common in some parts of India – it has a whiter colour and more robust flavour.

A word of caution: it's better to opt for ghee made in small batches rather than commercial volumes. The 'what happens in the factory, stays in the factory' secret to making ghee is old butter; it's difficult to get rid of butter close to its sell-by date, so it's sometimes turned into ghee. During this process, shortcuts can be taken, and factors such as overcooking, scorching, adulteration with vegetable oil, and oxidation due to poor packaging can affect quality.

Good ghee is golden-yellow to deep amber and clear when melted. It is opaque and creamy when set, although grainy crystals can form naturally (a sign of slow, traditional cooking). Its taste is rich, rounded and slightly sweet with a nutty depth.

Poor-quality ghee will be pale (suggesting poor-quality butter) or too dark or burnt, with a stale, waxy, soapy or burnt aroma. Its texture may be oily slick or chalky with a separation of fat and residue, and its taste neutral, greasy or bitter. It may not solidify properly when cool. A good rule of thumb is to avoid ghee sold in plastic jars or tubs.

CHURNING BUTTER

The earliest churn was little more than a goatskin, shaken by hand or strapped to an animal on the move. Nomadic peoples in Asia would shake bags of cream until butter formed. You can recreate the same at home without the animal skin - instead, half fill a clean jar with cream and shake, shake, shake until it turns to butter. Voila!

Over the centuries, people have invented countless versions of the butter churn, moving from the humble animal-skin bag to gleaming industrial machines that command the attention of the butter production room in which they stand.

I once ordered a churn over the internet, only to receive a large metal box the size of a dining table with a paddle inside. It was as loud as a Harley Davidson and we couldn't stay in the same room as it. Buyer, beware!

Today, there are two main ways to churn butter - continuous and batch.

Continuous churning

This is a system built for speed and efficiency. Introduced in the mid-twentieth century, this industrial process pushes cream through a line of machines where it is heated, churned, separated, worked and packaged in one seamless stream. The outcome is plentiful, consistent and suited to large-scale dairies supplying supermarkets and exporting to the other side of the world. These machines rarely stop, and cream turns to butter in three to five minutes, producing hundreds to thousands of kilograms of butter an hour. The majority of butter sold at supermarkets is produced with this method.

BELOW *Dairymen's Cooperative Creamery workers in Caldwell, Idaho, removing butter from a batch churn in 1941*
OPPOSITE LEFT *A barrel churn in Pennsylvania in the 1930s*
OPPOSITE RIGHT *A dash churn in a Kentucky home in 1940*

Batch churning

Batch churning is a more traditional form of butter-making and the method used by artisans today. Cream is churned in batches ranging from 20–3000 litres. Cream is poured into a churn, usually a rotating drum or barrel, and agitated until the fat globules collide and join together. As the butter grains form, the buttermilk is released and drained away. The butter is washed with cold, filtered water and then gently 'worked' to smooth the texture while also removing excess moisture.

It is a slower process, often taking 30–60 minutes, but gives the maker far more control. Cream can be fermented for longer, churned more slowly, or worked more carefully to bring out depths of flavour and a supple texture. The result is butter with more personality and the results tend to reflect season, quality of cream and style of recipe – all which are evident when it is tasted.

Dash and rocker churns

The dash churn was a farmhouse staple for centuries. Designed as a tall, narrow wooden or stone vessel with a lid, it had a wooden plunger, known as the dash, which was worked up and down by hand to agitate the cream. It was slow physical work, but it got results and was very popular among families with a house cow or two.

The more sophisticated version was the rocker or swing churn, where the vessel was suspended from a timber frame and rocked from side to side. You would be forgiven for thinking it was a baby bassinette in the kitchen of a farmhouse in the 1600s.

Barrel churns

By the 1800s, barrel churns had become popular. These were built like small wine barrels mounted in cradles made of wood. Controlled by a hand crank, the churn could process larger amounts of cream more efficiently. Some even had small windows so the butter-maker could peek in to see how the butter was coming along.

Tin, stoneware and glass churns

As the nineteenth century progressed, churns diversified. Tin churns and decorated stoneware models became common. Glass churns, often fitted with hand cranks and, later, electric motors, were especially popular in households from the 1800s through to the mid-twentieth century. Companies such as Dazey in the United States became famous for their churns, producing everything from one-quart jars to 10-gallon electrics.

Churning butter at home today

Today, glass churns are available for home butter-makers in the form of the Kilner Butter Churner. These are great for making small batches of butter for a few servings. The glass churn comes with a handle and paddles, making the experience mess free. For the novice, hand beaters, electric beaters or a stand mixer will work fine (although can be very messy!) when you're starting off. Food processors aren't great – remember that you want to agitate the cream rather than chop through it.

Stainless-steel churns

Today's batch churns are built from stainless steel, a shift driven by food safety standards and advances in technology. The traditional wooden barrels are only found in vintage stores, museums or historical displays, charming as they are. The steel design used by artisans today ensures better hygiene, durability and precise control over the butter-making process, all of which helps deliver a premium product.

ABOVE Butter being removed from a modern churn at Lard Ass Butter

BUTTERMILK

If you've only ever known supermarket 'cultured buttermilk', prepare to meet the real thing – tangy, silky, versatile and rooted in butter-making history.

Traditional cultured buttermilk is the liquid that drains away when cream is turned into butter. It's naturally fermented, slightly tart, beautifully smooth and almost fat-free. Long before fridges, its acidity made it safe to drink and easy to keep.

Historically, buttermilk sat at the centre of farmhouse cooking. It tenderised meats, gave lift to scones and soda breads, enriched soups and provided daily nourishment. It was also used in cheese-making, animal feed and even skincare. Buttermilk was valued because it was reliable, nutritious and endlessly adaptable.

In many cultures, it was served as a drink. Cold buttermilk was a refreshing summer staple in Europe, while in India, spiced buttermilk (chaas) is still beloved. Over in the American South, entire baking traditions were built around its gentle acidity.

Unfortunately, traditional buttermilk is often not what you find at the supermarket. Modern commercial buttermilk is typically skim milk powder that's been inoculated with cultures to mimic the flavour and acidity of the real thing. It works in recipes but it doesn't have the same depth or subtle buttery aroma that true buttermilk carries from the churn.

Thankfully, true buttermilk is currently enjoying a full-blown revival, thanks to chefs, bakers and home cooks rediscovering its character as one of the most useful, flavour-driven ingredients you can have on hand. Its acidity tenderises chicken for perfect fried chicken, lightens cakes and quick breads, enriches mashed potatoes and makes dressings, dips and marinades sing.

In modern pastry kitchens, it's used to balance sweetness, add complexity and bring a cultured tang to desserts. Think buttermilk panna cotta, ice cream, waffles, cheesecakes and doughnuts.

Best of all, when you have access to real buttermilk straight from the churn, you get a depth and freshness that no manufactured version can match. It tastes of the cream it came from, the cultures that transformed it and the hands that churned it. It connects the old and the new, bridging farmhouse thrift with modern culinary creativity: nothing is wasted, everything has character and even the 'leftovers' have a story of their own.

Speaking of leftovers, if you find yourself with too much buttermilk, it has a quiet second life in the garden. Its natural acidity and gentle nutrient profile make it an excellent fertiliser for plants that love slightly acidic soil – think hydrangeas, camellias, azaleas, blueberries and roses. Real buttermilk carries traces of lactic cultures, calcium, proteins and sugars that feed soil microbes and boost overall soil health. Diluted with water and poured around the base of plants, it acts like a mild tonic, encouraging stronger root systems, richer blooms and improved soil structure.

For storage, buttermilk freezes beautifully. Whether it's real buttermilk from the churn or the kind from the supermarket, it can be frozen for up to three months without losing its tang or usefulness. The texture may separate slightly once thawed, but a quick shake or whisk brings it back together. Freeze it in ice-cube trays or small containers for easy portions, and use it in baking, marinades, dressings, soups and the garden.

SWEET CREAM AND CULTURED BUTTER

The beauty of butter lies in its simplicity – it's just cream that's been churned. But the variety of butters around the world obviously tells a much richer story. The flavour, texture and colour of butter change depending on the cream used – whether it was cultured or sweet, the way it was churned and even the animal's diet. But, put most simply, there are two main types of butter: sweet cream butter and cultured butter.

Sweet cream butter

This butter is made from pasteurised cream and considered 'sweet' because of its lactose (milk sugar) content. Its flavour is heavily dependent on the quality and freshness of the cream. Sweet cream butter is available in salted or unsalted varieties. Unsalted sweet cream butter is considered the gold standard for pastry chefs, as it allows them to control a recipe's salt content.

Cultured butter (also called European butter)

The favourite of artisan butter-makers, this is made from cream that has been fermented before churning, giving the butter a slightly tangy, more complex flavour and a silkier texture. Because it is typically produced with a higher milk fat content, cultured butter is often referred to as European-style butter. This is the style made at Lard Ass, and in much of Europe.

When bacteria are added to cream in a warm environment, the magic starts and the warm cream becomes a living system. Acidity or pH is where flavour is formed, and in dairy fermentation the pH is encouraged to fall from neutral (7) to acidic (4.5–5.0). It's a quiet transformation, but one that gives butter its depth. Most of the magic comes from the production of diacetyl, the molecule that smells like warm, buttered popcorn. It's joined by acetoin and dozens of other compounds that layer subtle flavours: nutty, tangy, sometimes even floral.

Setting the length of fermentation is like setting the dial on flavour intensity. A short ripening gives a light, fresh butter. Let it run longer and you get tangier, more complex butter. Fermentation is the reason why cultured butter feels fuller in the mouth and lingers longer on the palate – you're tasting the flavour chemistry.

Traditional farmhouse culturing was as much art as it was science – a process guided by seasons, personal taste, instinct and the natural bacteria in the dairy. Each batch carried the character of the farm, the cows and the time of year.

By contrast, modern culturing is about quick turnaround, control and consistency. Defined starter cultures, temperature regulation and pH monitoring ensure the flavour is predictable and safe, and season is more hinderance than help.

The flavour, traditionally produced by slow-culturing the cream over 24 hours, is now often derived by adding a powder or liquid starter distillate to the already-churned butter. Today, big commercial companies identify these flavour add-ins as 'natural flavours' or 'lactic acid' on their labels. They're the same flavour compounds often used to give buttered popcorn its signature taste.

While this process delivers the familiar 'cultured' aroma, it doesn't develop the same depth of character or the rich, rounded mouthfeel as natural fermentation. Many commercial brands use this process – also known as the NIZO butter process – to avoid the time and complexity of fermenting cream. It also creates more stability – meaning less spoilage and sensitivity to variation.

Both approaches have their charm: one celebrates variation and terroir, the other guarantees a reliable flavour every time. There's a place for everything.

CARING FOR BUTTER

Butter is like a living thing. It speaks to you – figuratively speaking, of course – and responds to the world around it. It softens in the warmth, hardens in the cold, glows in good light or turns dull when neglected. It holds within it the memory of the cream it came from – the pastures, the season, the cows – and this shows in its flavour. It deserves to be treated with care. As with most fats, butter is sensitive to its surroundings.

It's not a cheap product, so looking after your butter is an act of respect, preserving what makes it special: the flavour, texture and overall mouthfeel. The way it is stored, what it is stored in or with, and even the knife you use to spread it will influence how your butter behaves when it arrives at the table.

At its heart, butter is an emulsion: a blend of fat and water bound harmoniously. That balance is what gives butter its silkiness, its ability to melt evenly and its remarkable flavour-carrying power.

Like most of us, butter has some vulnerabilities. There are three things it dislikes above all else: air, light and swings in temperature.

Air dries out its surface and causes oxidation, dulling its flavour and removing its colour. Light fades its natural golden tones and accelerates rancidity, especially sunlight or fluorescent light. Opaque containers made are best for storing butter – beware of handsome clear glass butter dishes. They're suitable for anything but butter.

Temperature fluctuations break butter's storage rhythm. Moving butter repeatedly from fridge to benchtop makes it sweat and lose structure, and can cause rancidity too. Try to be consistent when storing butter, ensuring its home is always cool, dry and calm.

ABOVE Kat of Lard Ass Butter handling a butter sheet after forming

WRAPPING AND STORING BUTTER

From homemade butter balls to our familiar supermarket staple, packaging is critical – butter hates air, light and temperature fluctuations, and there's no coming back from rancid or spoiled butter.

Parchment paper

Breathable, biodegradable and nostalgic – parchment is traditional but not the best at blocking out air or odours. Best for short shelf life or small-batch artisan butters.

Butter foil

The gold standard for quality butter packaging and the most popular today, butter foil combines the charm of foil-wrapped blocks with excellent protection against light and air. It keeps flavour intact longer, which is why you'll see it wrapping most commercial butters.

Tin cans

Once popular in Scandinavia and still used in parts of the Middle East, butter-in-a-can is practical for long-term storage (especially clarified butter). Airtight and lightproof, but a bit old-fashioned for modern consumers.

Glass jars

Not a commercial option but a convenient choice for home butter-makers. Jars are a great idea if you are giving butter as gifts. They show off colour and texture, but they're heavy, fragile and costly, and clear glass does not protect butter from light. More of a boutique option than a practical one.

Plastic tubs

Practical and inexpensive, plastic tubs are easy to reseal and stack neatly in the fridge. However, they're more often associated with margarine and spreadable blends than with premium butter and, while handy, they let in some oxygen over time and don't win points with eco-conscious customers.

Benchtop, fridge or freezer?

There's a fine balance between keeping butter safe from spoiling and keeping it spreadable. Butter can happily sit out in a butter dish at room temperature for two to five days, or more in cooler weather, provided it is kept covered and away from direct light. In summer, or in warm kitchens, it's best stored in the fridge and brought to room temperature as needed. I always recommend keeping the butter dish in a place in your kitchen where the temperature is mild, such as the pantry.

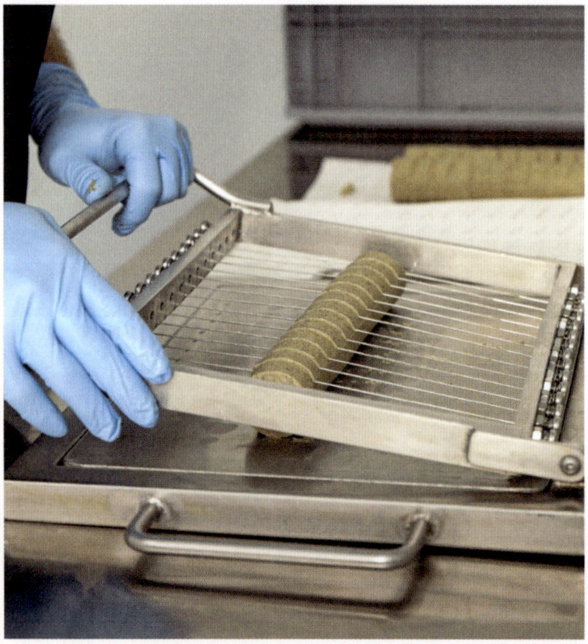

ABOVE AND OPPOSITE Butter being prepared for packaging

As a rule of thumb, butter keeps for one to three months in the fridge - salted or unsalted, opened or unopened - so long as it's well wrapped. For the best, clean flavour, keep it airtight and away from pungent neighbours (such as onions, garlic, and blue cheese). Store it in its wrapper inside an airtight container or foil layer to block air and light.

Butter is so effective at absorbing scent that it was used to capture and hold fragrance in the early days of perfume-making. That little detail says everything about how sensitive butter is and why it deserves thoughtful storage. Even your fridge agrees: that special compartment marked 'Butter' is proof enough that it deserves its own space.

For longer storage, freeze it. Most butter around the world is frozen prior to reaching its retail destination and we are none the wiser. Wrap yours in foil, parchment or freezer-safe paper, then seal it inside a container or ziplock bag to prevent freezer burn. Commercially made butter can rest this way for up to 12 months. When you are ready to use the butter, thaw it gently in the fridge - never in the microwave or on a hot benchtop. Slow thawing keeps its texture smooth and flavour uncompromised.

Refreezing butter is not advised. Once thawed, its emulsion weakens slightly, and refreezing may cause the butter to separate, creating small pockets of water. Off flavours can develop. Freeze your butter in small portions instead, so you can take out what you need and leave the rest undisturbed.

Storing salted versus unsalted

Not all butter behaves the same way in storage. Salted butter has a natural preservative advantage - the salt slows bacterial growth and oxidation, giving it a longer life both in the fridge and at room temperature. Unsalted butter, by contrast, is more fragile. The difference might seem small, but it's the reason bakers insist on unsalted butter - its flavour is clean and pure.

When butter goes bad

Regardless of the type of butter, it does eventually go bad. Fresh butter smells clean and sweet, with a gentle creaminess and no sharpness on the nose. Its colour is even and natural - golden in summer, pale in winter - and it should feel smooth and pliable, not sticky or greasy. When butter begins to 'turn', the change is unmistakable: the aroma grows sour or slightly metallic, the taste becomes flat or bitter and the surface may darken or develop uneven patches. This is rancidity - oxidation at work, as light and air begin to break down the fat.

While old butter isn't harmful in small amounts, it loses the pleasure of freshness. You can still use it for cooking, baking or frying where heat and other flavours mask the decline, but the magic of good butter lies in its brightness. Store it well, protect it from light and your butter will stay lively, fragrant and ready to shine.

BUTTER TOOLS

Last century, families would have had a kitchen cupboard full of butter-keeping implements and tools. Today you're lucky to find a suitable butter dish. However, if you dig a little deeper, you can find some equipment to help store and care for your butter.

Butter bell

I love a good butter dish, but another secret to keeping butter both fresh and perfectly spreadable lies in the clever design of the butter bell, also called a butter crock. Long before refrigeration, families stored their butter in simple earthenware pots – some large, some small – often sealed with a thin layer of water to keep out air and avoid spoilage. The water-submerged butter crock is believed to have first appeared in medieval France.

Not every French household used one, but those who did swore by its charm and practicality. Today, the butter bell is making a quiet comeback, loved by those who appreciate soft, ready-to-use butter without the need for refrigeration.

Each bell holds a stick or two of butter. You pack softened butter into the bell-shaped cup, then pour cold water into the base. The lid is placed upside-down into the base. The water creates an airtight seal that preserves the freshness of the butter while keeping it at room temperature.

Butter knife

The butter knife is one of the gentlest tools at the table. It doesn't slice or stab – it glides. Its purpose is to serve, to lift and to spread. The round and broad blade was borne out of weariness when, in the seventeenth century, France's Cardinal Richelieu grew tired of watching his dinner guests use the sharp tips of his knives to pick their teeth after a meal. He ordered a set of knives with their ends rounded off, creating the first table knives.

Butter curler

Another useful and very pretty tool is the butter curler. Once a staple of grand hotels and elegant dining rooms, it was used to scrape delicate curls from a cold block of butter, presenting small golden ribbons that softened perfectly on the plate. There is something undeniably pleasing about a bowl of butter curls served with a basket of bread rolls – especially if you have churned the butter yourself.

Butter baller

Very much like a melon baller or scoop, this tool can be used to form balls from chilled butter to serve with bread rolls. Before using, dip the scoop in hot water, then dry it, and keep your butter balls on a chilled, lined tray in the fridge. Butter balls are nice to make if you're serving flavoured butters (pages 74–89) for special occasions. For a ridged look, roll briefly across a cold butter paddle to make a decorative pattern.

Spoons for quenelles

Quenelles are spoon-shaped ovals with a satin surface, elegant on hot steaks, fish, vegetables or pancakes where they melt to make an instant sauce. They can be made from plain or compound butter and always look impressive. The only tool required is a pair of dessert spoons. Warm them in hot water and then dry. Lift slightly softened butter with one spoon, then pass it back and forth between the two spoons, smoothing and shaping into an oval. Set on a chilled, lined tray in the fridge until ready to serve.

Butter paddles

Also known as Scotch hands and gnocchi boards, these paddles are wooden spatulas used to 'work' butter after churning. The fresh butter is pressed with them to drive out any watery buttermilk and to knead in the salt evenly, which both slow down rancidity and extend shelf life. One face is ribbed or grooved, so liquid can drain as you press; the smooth face is for shaping the butter into its final form. The ridged pattern is the trademark signature of French artisan butter-maker Beurre Bordier.

Butter moulds

While artists like Caroline Shawk Brooks are famous for their butter-carving abilities, you can also make your own centrepiece with far less effort and skill. Available in a range of designs, moulds shape your butter, creating designs like lambs or impressions of flowers that are almost too pretty to slice a knife into. If you want to make a State Fair-sized cow, however, you may be out of luck.

BUTTERS OF THE WORLD

The beauty of butter is that – although its flavour, colour and traditions vary from country to country, reflecting climate, culture and traditions – there is one universal rule that is deeply respected: 'butter' must contain at least 80 per cent milk fat. Beyond that standard, each region puts its own stamp on its local butter.

French beurre d'Isigny

Butter-making is very serious business in France, so much so that several butter-making regions have been granted AOC (appellation d'origine contrôlée) or its European equivalent, PDO (protected designation of origin) status, meaning their butter must be produced, processed and prepared in a specific region using traditional methods. PGI (protected geographical indication) is more flexible, mandating at least one of the production stages must take place in the region.

From the Isigny region in Normandy, Beurre d'Isigny is made with milk from cows grazing on mineral-rich pastures. This butter is known for its deep golden colour, silky texture and naturally high carotene content. It often has a slight hazelnut flavour and a rich, creamy mouthfeel.

French beurre Charentes-Poitou

Produced in the Charentes and Poitou regions of western France, this is a cultured butter with a tangy flavour and supple texture. It's a favourite of French pastry chefs, especially for croissants and viennoiserie.

French beurre de Bresse

Made in the Bresse region, traditionally from pasture-fed cows, this butter is recognised for its sweet, delicate flavour and smooth texture. It is produced in small quantities, making it highly prized.

French beurre des Deux-Sèvres

From the Deux-Sèvres area in western France, this butter is known for its distinctive creamy, slightly grassy flavour.

French beurre de Baratte

Beurre de Baratte literally means 'butter of the churn', referring to the traditional wooden barrel churns still used by a few of its producers. These butters are usually made from cultured cream, giving them a delicate tang and rich aroma.

Danish butter

Danish butter, including the famous Lurpak, is known for its smooth texture and clean, sweet flavour. It is usually made from sweet cream rather than cultured cream, making it milder than its French cousins. Danish butter is highly consistent – pale yellow, with just enough salt to balance the richness – and has become a staple on tables across Europe.

Danish smör and kærnet smør

Kærnet smør, which translates to 'churned butter', is often made from cultured cream. It tends to have a subtle tang and a creamy consistency and, in some regions, it is still made in small dairies using wooden churns, preserving that old-world character.

Dutch butter

Dutch butter is traditionally made from cream produced by cows grazing on lush grassland meadows, giving it a creamy texture and natural yellow hue. Butter plays a central role in popular Dutch foods such as poffertjes, stroopwafels and boterkoek. While large co-operative producers underpin the country's supply, small regional makers such as Den Eelder emphasise quality and tradition.

New Zealand butter

Butter has been part of New Zealand's culinary life since nineteenth-century settlers arrived with European food traditions. With most dairy cows grazing on grass, butter is predominantly made as sweet cream butter, prized for its rich flavour and golden colour, with comparatively little emphasis on cultured European-style butters.

Irish butter

Ireland's butter is instantly recognisable by its deep yellow colour, a natural result of the carotene-rich grass that Irish cows graze on almost year-round. The flavour is sweet, creamy and slightly grassy – a reflection of the lush pastures. Irish butter has become so beloved that brands like Kerrygold have a global following, bringing that golden hue to kitchens around the world – particularly in the US.

Spanish butter

Spain's small but proud tradition of butter-making is kept alive with Lorenzana, dating back to 1920, and some of the small cheese-makers like Queixos Brigantia, who make a rich creamy butter from the Galicia region.

Nordic and Eastern European butter

Butter has a special place in Nordic and Eastern European kitchens, where it has long been a source of comfort through lengthy, cold winters. The styles here are often slightly tangy, reflecting the historic practice of letting cream sour naturally before churning, which gave butter a longer shelf life before refrigeration.

Finnish and Swedish cultured butter

In Sweden and Finland, butter is traditionally made from slightly soured cream, resulting in a gentle tang and a soft, spreadable texture. In Finland, voi (Finnish for butter) is often salted and eaten on dense rye bread, sometimes alongside pickled herring – a true taste of the region's food culture. Modern producers have maintained the tradition of lightly cultured butter.

Russian smetana butter

In Russia and across Eastern Europe, cream is often fermented into smetana (a rich, tangy cream similar to sour cream) before churning. This gives the resulting butter a bold cultured flavour and a slight sharpness that stands up beautifully to dark rye breads or hearty soups like borscht.

Polish masło

Polish masło (butter) is generally sold unsalted. Two types of butter are produced in Poland: ekstra, which is made from pasteurised, naturally fermented cream and packaged in aluminium coated parchment paper, and śmietankowe, made from non-fermented cream and packaged in printed parchment.

North American sweet cream butter

Butter in North America reflects the influence of European dairy traditions but has developed its own character – often paler, milder and focused on versatility. In recent years, as in the UK and Australia, there has been a welcomed revival of small-scale, cultured butter-making which has seen the return of some of the complexity lost to industrial production.

Most butter in the US and Canada is made from sweet cream – fresh, unfermented cream – giving it a mild, milky flavour and pale colour. These characteristics make it incredibly versatile for cooking and baking.

Latin American mantequilla

In Mexico and across Latin America mantequilla (Spanish for butter) is widely used for cooking, spreading and baking. In some regions, cream is lightly soured before churning. Its flavour can range from sweet and creamy to robust and earthy, depending on local dairy traditions.

Himalayan yak butter

High in the Himalayas, in China and Nepal, yak butter is made from yak's milk cream, churned by hand or using a tall wooden churn. The butter is highly aromatic, with a strong tang and grassy notes that reflect the yak's mountain pasture diet. Its most famous use is in yak butter tea (po cha), made by blending the butter with hot tea and salt to make a warming, calorie-dense drink that helps the locals withstand the harsh cold.

Chinese su-you

In parts of western China, a clarified butter known as su-you is used in traditional pastries and noodles, lending them a distinctive richness. Like ghee, it keeps well at room temperature and is an important cooking fat in regions with limited refrigeration.

Middle-Eastern samna

In Egypt, Sudan and across parts of the Middle East, clarified butter is known as samna (or samneh). Sometimes it is fermented before clarification, resulting in a strong, tangy, cheesy flavour that adds depth to savoury dishes. Spices such as fenugreek or cardamom are occasionally added to create a fragrant, golden cooking fat.

Buffalo milk butter

Though less common than cow's milk butter, buffalo milk butter is a delicacy in parts of Italy. Made from the same milk used for mozzarella di bufala, this butter is almost pure white, with a rich, sweet flavour and a silky texture. It is prized for delicate sauces or simply spread on crusty bread with a pinch of sea salt. Try Delitia Butter and Fattorie Garofalo's Burro di Bufala, both from Italy.

Goat or sheep butter

Less common than cow's butter, but worth the search as these butters have distinctive flavours. Goat butter is pure white and slightly grassy, while sheep butter is sharper and funkier. While less creamy, the overall taste is very prominent, although it can come across as mildly rancid at times. For goat butter, try Caldermeade Farm (Australia), St Helen's Farm (UK) and Delamere Dairy (UK). For sheep butter, try Spring Sheep Milk Co (NZ), Secret Lands Farm (Canada) and Cellagrande (Italy).

Whey butter

Whey butter is not made from cream, but from the fat that rises to the surface of whey during cheese-making. This style of butter is especially common in northern Italy, where it is a natural by-product of the region's famous hard cheeses such as Parmigiano Reggiano and Grana Padano. This deeply flavoured butter has a rich, nutty and slightly cheesy flavour with a less shiny, firmer texture than regular butter. It can vary in colour depending on the type of cheese being produced. Try Vannella Cheese (Australia), Quicke's Lady Prue Whey Butter and Slightly Salted Grass Fed Whey Butter (UK), Longman Farmhouse Whey Butter (UK) and Moinear Whey Cream Butter (USA).

Plant-based butters

Plant-based butters are designed to mimic the flavour, texture and performance of dairy butter, using vegetable fats such as coconut oil, shea butter, sunflower oil or blends of plant oils. Advances in food technology have made them creamier and more convincing than ever, allowing them to spread, melt and even brown much like traditional butter. While some are flavoured and coloured to resemble sweet cream butter, others are cultured with lactic acid bacteria to replicate the tang of cultured dairy butter. Plant-based butters have become a welcome option for vegans and those with dairy allergies.

Engineered butter

Not all butter is made to be eaten on warm bread. Some is made to behave – in factories, in food science labs and on supermarket shelves. Fractionated butter is one of these. This is butter that's been taken apart and separated into – usually two – different fat fractions: olein fats or soft fats, and stearin fats or hard fats. These fats are then put back together in a way that suits industry needs. Think chocolate coatings that won't melt too quickly, spreads that stay soft in the fridge, or baked goods that need a very specific texture, or to stay firm on a warm day.

It's no surprise then that around 99 per cent of the world's commercial bakers use this kind of butter to make their croissants, Danish pastries and pies. Thanks to modern technology, this type of butter is highly reliable and delivers the same result every time – consistent lift, flaky layers and controlled melting. It's predictable, efficient and designed for performance.

But, while fractionation makes for reliable pastry, it comes at the cost of flavour. When those soft olein fats are removed, so is the natural buttery flavour, and the natural colour or betacarotene that was found in a cow's diet.

The stearin fats are the hard fats that give butter its structure and firmness. Their taste is neutral, and they lack colour and don't contain as many of the volatile compounds that sit in softer fats. Essentially, stearin fats are valued for functionality such as giving puff pastry its strength or chocolate coating its ability not to melt.

A baker using pure, unmodified butter must adjust to its seasons: firmer in winter, softer in summer, unpredictable day to day. It is a live product, and their skill lies in sensing the butter's mood and coaxing it into lamination, folding, shaping and baking. It's an art that requires patience and touch.

Engineered butter provides predictability and consistency, much like a bag of sliced white bread. It's designed to behave the same way every time, eliminating the variables that challenge a baker's craft. It offers speed, reliability and less waste – qualities prized in commercial kitchens.

Fractionated butter is the baker's friend for control and convenience, but the artisan's enemy when it comes to flavour and soul.

MAKING YOUR OWN BUTTER

MAKING *your own* BUTTER

. . .

There is something deeply grounding about making butter at home. It's a simple act – cream plus movement plus time – but one that connects you instantly to centuries of dairy craft. Making butter is one of the most satisfying kitchen skills you can learn and, when you make it yourself, you will find you are more conscious of not wasting it!

When it comes to making butter at home, you need only consider three simple things: freshness of cream, flavour through salting, and storage.

Making butter all starts with choosing the right cream. Good butter can only come from good cream. For home churning, look for pure fresh cream with a fat content of at least 35 per cent (see page 41 for suitable creams). The higher the fat, the better the yield and the richer the flavour. I always recommend using pure pasteurised cream with nothing added – no gums, no stabilisers, no thickeners. The cleaner the cream, the cleaner and brighter your butter will taste.

Avoid ultra-pasteurised cream, which has been heated to very high temperatures and won't whip well. It tends to stay stubbornly liquid or turns greasy instead of forming proper butter granules.

Also avoid 'thickened cream', which often contains gelatine or vegetable gums to give it body. Those additives interfere with the whipping process and affect the texture of the finished butter.

Freshness matters, too. Cream that's very old or close to its expiry date won't whip or separate as predictably. If you're making cultured or kefir butter, in particular, be sure to use cream that has plenty of life left in it so the fermentation has room to develop flavour without tipping into sourness.

Once the butter forms, it is washed in very cold water until the liquid runs clear. This removes any residual buttermilk, helping the butter last longer and taste fresher.

Don't be afraid of the process. Butter wants to happen – it's simply a matter of taking cream a little further than whipped cream. With the right ingredients and a bit of patience, homemade butter is one of the great kitchen pleasures.

Once you have fresh butter in your hands, the next question is always the same: to salt or not to salt? Unsalted is great for baking and for tasting the pure flavour of the cream. But salt brings the butter to life – enhancing richness, balancing sweetness and extending the shelf life slightly. Start with 0.8–1.5 per cent salt by weight and adjust to your taste. You can even go a step further and use rock salt or salt flakes for texture, or coloured salt such as pink or black sea salt for an eye-catching look.

Sweet cream butter

This is the simplest and most familiar butter to most people – cream goes straight into the mixer and becomes much more. The flavour is clean, fresh and slightly milky. Your butter won't taste 'buttery' because sweet cream is alkaline, meaning no flavour and no odour. It's a perfect canvas for salt or flavours. Sweet cream butter can be made at any time of the year, but the results are likely to change with every batch, due to season, temperature, quality of cream and degree of agitation.

▪ ▪ ▪ MAKES 250–300 G (9–10½ OZ) BUTTER PLUS 200 ML (7 FL OZ) BUTTERMILK ▪ ▪ ▪

1 litre (4 cups) pasteurised cream with minimum 35% fat (see page 41)
1 litre (4 cups) ice-cold water
½–1 teaspoon sea salt, to taste

Remove the cream from the fridge 30 minutes before you start, so it warms up a little to make it ideal for whipping. If the cream is too cold, it will take too long to whip. The Goldilocks zone is 10–13°C (50–55°F), where the cream churns smoothly and breaks cleanly into butter and buttermilk.

Pour the cream into the bowl of a stand mixer, or use electric beaters or hand beaters, and beat for 4–6 minutes on medium–high until it becomes whipped cream and reaches firm peaks.

Keep going for another 1–3 minutes, until it separates into butterfat and buttermilk; to avoid the buttermilk splattering, you can cover the mixer with a tea towel. Once the fat separates and clumps together, stop immediately. Pour off the liquid buttermilk and save it for baking or pancakes – store the buttermilk in a sealed jar in the fridge for up to 1 week, or freeze for longer (see page 49).

Transfer the butter to a separate bowl. Add about half of the ice-cold water and gently knead or stir the butter to rinse away any remaining buttermilk. Repeat this rinsing with the remaining water until it runs clear – this helps your butter stay fresh longer.

Knead until smooth, working out any remaining moisture. Add salt if desired; start with ½ teaspoon and adjust to taste. Shape the butter into blocks or rolls, wrap and refrigerate.

Store the butter wrapped in baking paper or parchment paper in the fridge for up to 2 weeks, or freeze for up to 3 months in an airtight container.

Cultured butter

Cultured butter is the flavour of farmhouse kitchens, alpine dairies and old-fashioned churns – and it's surprisingly easy to make at home with very little equipment. If you use buttermilk here, the butter will have a slightly milder tang, while yoghurt adds a creamier note. The cultured buttermilk from this process makes amazing pancakes, soda bread and marinades.

▪ ▪ ▪ MAKES 350–450 G (12½ OZ–1 LB) BUTTER PLUS 500 ML (17 FL OZ) BUTTERMILK ▪ ▪ ▪

- 1 litre (4 cups) pasteurised cream with minimum 35% fat (see page 41)
- 2 tablespoons natural live yoghurt or cultured buttermilk (with active cultures)
- 1 litre (4 cups) ice-cold water
- ½–1 teaspoon sea salt, to taste

Pour the cream into a clean glass or ceramic jar. Stir in the yoghurt until completely combined. Cover with a clean cloth or loose lid and leave to sit at room temperature (20–22°C/68–72°F) for 12–18 hours, until the cream is slightly thickened and pleasantly tangy, like a light sour cream or crème fraîche.

Place the cultured thickened cream in the fridge for 2 hours to cool it; cold cream churns more cleanly and produces firmer butter with a bolder flavour. The Goldilocks zone is 10–13°C (50–55°F), where the cream churns smoothly and breaks cleanly into butter and buttermilk.

Pour the cream into the bowl of a stand mixer, or use electric beaters or hand beaters, and beat for 2–6 minutes until the butterfat clumps together and separates from the buttermilk; to avoid the buttermilk splattering, you can cover the mixer with a tea towel.

Once the fat separates and clumps together, stop immediately. Pour off the liquid buttermilk and save it for baking or pancakes – store the buttermilk in a sealed jar in the fridge for up to 1 week, or freeze for longer (see page 49).

Transfer the butter to a separate bowl. Add about half of the ice-cold water and gently knead or stir the butter to rinse away any remaining buttermilk. Repeat this rinsing with the remaining water until it runs clear – this helps your butter stay fresh longer.

Knead until smooth, working out any remaining moisture. Add salt if desired; start with ½ teaspoon and adjust to taste. Shape the butter into blocks or rolls, wrap and refrigerate.

Store the butter wrapped in baking paper or parchment paper in the fridge for up to 2 weeks, or freeze for up to 3 months in an airtight container.

2:30pm
11/03
16oz
400ml
2Cups
1½Cups
1Cup
½Cup

Kefir butter

Kefir butter has a gentle tang and a beautiful depth of flavour. While you can use store-bought kefir, using live grains to make your kefir gives this butter the most authentic result – the grains ferment the cream slowly and naturally, producing a flavour you simply can't get from powdered cultures. Kefir grains can often be found through local fermentation groups, community food swaps, online marketplaces, or shared among home fermenters who are always happy to pass some on.

▪ ▪ ▪ MAKES 350–450 G (12½ OZ–1 LB) BUTTER PLUS 500 ML (17 FL OZ) BUTTERMILK ▪ ▪ ▪

1 litre (4 cups) pasteurised cream with minimum 35% fat (see page 41)
3 tablespoons kefir with live cultures or ¼ teaspoon kefir grains
1 litre (4 cups) ice-cold water
½–1 teaspoon sea salt, to taste

Pour the cream into a clean glass or ceramic jar and stir in the kefir. Cover with a clean cloth or loose lid and leave to sit at room temperature (20–22°C/68–72°F) for 12–24 hours, until slightly thickened and pleasantly tangy, like a light sour cream or crème fraîche. If you are using kefir grains, scoop out the grains and store them in a sealed glass jar with a plastic or glass lid in the fridge for reuse.

Refrigerate the cream for 2 hours to cool it; cold cream churns cleanly and produces firmer butter with a bolder flavour. The Goldilocks zone is 10–13°C (50–55°F), where the cream churns smoothly and breaks cleanly into butter and buttermilk.

Pour the cream into the bowl of a stand mixer, or use electric beaters or hand beaters, and beat for 2–6 minutes until the butterfat clumps together and separates from the buttermilk; to avoid the buttermilk splattering, you can cover the mixer with a tea towel.

Once the fat separates and clumps together, stop immediately. Pour off the liquid buttermilk and save it for baking or pancakes – store the buttermilk in a sealed jar in the fridge for up to 1 week, or freeze for longer (see page 49).

Transfer the butter to a separate bowl. Add about half of the ice-cold water and gently knead or stir to rinse away any remaining buttermilk. Repeat this rinsing until the water runs clear – this helps your butter stay fresh longer.

Knead until smooth, working out any remaining moisture. Add salt if desired; start with ½ teaspoon and adjust to taste. Shape the butter into blocks or rolls, wrap and refrigerate.

Store the butter wrapped in baking paper or parchment paper in the fridge for up to 2 weeks, or freeze for up to 3 months in an airtight container.

Ghee

Making ghee is a deeply satisfying kitchen activity. Come armed with a heavy-based saucepan and some good butter and you will be handsomely rewarded. Look at this as a process of distilling butter to its essence.

You can use ghee for cooking and baking in place of butter. Use 185 ml (¾ cup) ghee in place of 250 ml (1 cup) butter to achieve a nutty, toasty flavour and crumbly texture for biscuits, cakes, pastry, muffins and breads. When you use ghee during baking, you might need to add a couple of tablespoons of water for moisture, too.

▪ ▪ ▪ MAKES 400 ML (AROUND 14 FL OZ) ▪ ▪ ▪

500 g (1 lb 2 oz) unsalted cultured butter

Place the butter in a heavy-based saucepan over low–medium heat. Let it melt slowly, without rushing it. Soon you'll see a pale foam forming on the surface – that's the water evaporating.

Let it simmer gently until the butter begins to separate into three layers: foam on top, clear golden liquid in the middle and milk solids sinking to the bottom. Keep the heat gentle – you're coaxing the water out, not frying the solids. There is no need to stir or skim the solids away from the top of the ghee; they will settle to the bottom as the water evaporates.

After 10–20 minutes the milk solids will turn a light caramel brown and the bubbling will slow. The kitchen will fill with a nutty, toffee-like scent, letting you know your ghee is ready. Keep an eye on the pan, as you want to be careful not to burn the solids.

Remove the pan from the heat and let it cool for a few minutes. Pour the liquid through a fine strainer lined with muslin into a clean dry bowl. Discard the milk solids, or see Notes for a great way to use them. Leave the ghee to cool to room temperature.

Pour the cooled ghee into a clean glass jar to store. It will be golden and clear, then set softly as it cools.

Store the ghee at room temperature for up to a year, or for even longer in the fridge; if the ghee discolours or its smell changes, dispose of it.

Notes

To learn more about ghee, and the difference between it and clarified butter, flip to page 44

Thanks to a customer, I finally discovered a way to use those nutty, sweet leftovers! Simply combine 200 g (1 cup) of the milk solids with 3 tablespoons peanut butter (I like crunchy), 3 tablespoons maple syrup, agave syrup or honey, and 60 g (½ cup) sultanas, cranberries or chopped dried apricots. Mix the ingredients together, press into a baking tin lined with baking paper and chill in the fridge for 1 hour. Cut into squares and enjoy as a snack.

FLAVOURED BUTTER

Also known as 'compound butter', flavoured butter is simply butter plus well-chosen additions, mixed and chilled. In French cooking it's often considered a finishing sauce. Butter absorbs aromas like a sponge, which makes it the perfect vehicle for herbs, spices or almost any of your favourite ingredients. One disc of flavoured butter is enough to transform anything it touches, turning a plain chicken breast or a piece of fish into something you can proudly serve.

The original celebrity of the style is beurre maître d'hôtel – parsley and lemon worked into soft butter, then set on a hot steak so it melts as the meat rests. The herbs and citrus lift the richness, adding brightness without fuss.

In today's flavoured butter revival, ingredients like miso, harissa, gochujang, nori and pepperberry create clear, contemporary flavours. With quality butter and good ingredients at hand – fresh herbs, citrus zest, garlic, miso, anchovies – you can roll a log on Sunday and have a week's worth of instant upgrades ready in the fridge. The variations are endless. Here are some of my favourite combinations to try at home – simple to make, endlessly adaptable and always better when made with good butter.

▪ ▪ ▪

To shape your roll, spoon your flavoured butter onto a sheet of baking paper, roll it into a log about 2.5 cm (1 in) thick, and twist the ends to seal. Once chilled, you can slice off pieces as needed or pre-cut your logs so you can grab a portion from the freezer when you need it. Or, for easy scooping, store your butter in a small airtight container.

You should chill your flavoured butters for at least 1 hour before using.

Flavoured butters will keep refrigerated in an airtight container for up to 2 weeks or frozen for up to 3 months.

Garlic butter

▪ ▪ ▪ SERVES 4 ▪ ▪ ▪

150 g (5½ oz) salted butter, softened
2–3 garlic cloves, minced
15 g (½ cup) flat-leaf parsley, finely sliced
zest of one lemon

In a bowl, mix all the ingredients into the butter until well combined. Season with salt and pepper.

▪ ▪ ▪

Enjoy with steaks or burgers fresh off the grill, roasted chicken, seafood, pasta, your favourite vegetables, scrambled eggs or warm bread.

Herb and garlic butter

▪ ▪ ▪ SERVES 4 ▪ ▪ ▪

150 g (5½ oz) salted butter, softened
½ teaspoon dried garlic granules
½ tablespoon dried onion flakes
½ tablespoon finely chopped parsley
½ tablespoon finely chopped chives
1 teaspoon finely chopped oregano
1 teaspoon finely chopped thyme
1 teaspoon chopped capers (optional)

In a bowl, mix all the ingredients into the butter until well combined.

▪ ▪ ▪

Enjoy with roasted or fried chicken, scrambled eggs, warm bread, your favourite vegetables or grilled or pan-seared white fish.

Lemon dill butter

▪ ▪ ▪ SERVES 4 ▪ ▪ ▪

150 g (5½ oz) salted butter, softened
1 tablespoon finely chopped dill
2 teaspoons lemon zest
1 tablespoon lemon juice
¼ teaspoon salt

In a bowl, mix all the ingredients into the butter until well combined.

▪ ▪ ▪

Enjoy with baked fish, prawns (shrimp), steak or chicken fresh off the grill, or potatoes.

Rosemary butter

▪ ▪ ▪ SERVES 4 ▪ ▪ ▪

150 g (5½ oz) salted butter, softened
3 garlic cloves, minced
2 tablespoons finely chopped rosemary leaves
½ teaspoon cracked black pepper
½ teaspoon lemon zest
¼ teaspoon lemon juice

In a bowl, mix all the ingredients, except the lemon juice, into the butter until well combined. Add the juice and mix again.

▪ ▪ ▪

Enjoy with steak by itself or on a sandwich, roasted chicken, potatoes or other vegetables of your choice.

Parsley butter

▪ ▪ ▪ SERVES 4 ▪ ▪ ▪

150 g (5½ oz) salted butter, softened
2 teaspoons chopped parsley leaves
1 teaspoon Worcestershire sauce
¼ teaspoon lemon juice

In a bowl, mix all the ingredients into the butter until well combined.

▪ ▪ ▪

Enjoy with steak or fish fresh off the grill, potatoes, roasted chicken, omelettes or scrambled eggs.

Ploughgate Creamery's chive flower butter

▪ ▪ ▪ SERVES 4 ▪ ▪ ▪

150 g (5½ oz) cultured butter, softened
2–3 tablespoons finely chopped chives
2–3 tablespoons chive flowers, individual petals only

In a bowl, mix all the ingredients into the butter until well combined, adjusting the ratio of chives and petals to taste.

▪ ▪ ▪

Enjoy with warm bread, fresh oysters, your favourite vegetables or on a charcuterie board.

Shallot and tarragon butter

▪ ▪ ▪ SERVES 4 ▪ ▪ ▪

150 g (5½ oz) salted butter, softened
100 g (3½ oz) French shallots, finely chopped
25 g (1 oz) finely chopped tarragon leaves
1 tablespoon lemon juice

In a saucepan over low heat, melt 25 g (1 oz) of the butter. Add the shallots and saute for 10 minutes, until very soft but not coloured. Allow to cool.

Mix the cooled shallots into the remaining butter with the tarragon and lemon juice. Season with pepper.

▪ ▪ ▪

Enjoy with steak fresh off the grill, potatoes, warm chapati or Turkish bread, lamb chops, corn on the cob, roasted chicken or fries.

Shallots and red wine reduction butter

▪ ▪ ▪ SERVES 4 ▪ ▪ ▪

150 g (5½ oz) salted butter, softened, plus 2 tablespoons
40 g (¼ cup) French shallots, finely chopped
1 tablespoon finely chopped tarragon or sage
1 tablespoon finely chopped garlic
125 ml (½ cup) red wine, such as cabernet sauvignon
½ tablespoon finely chopped parsley

In a saucepan over medium-low heat, melt the 2 tablespoons of butter. Add the shallots and saute them for a few minutes, until they are translucent and light golden brown. Add the tarragon and garlic and cook for about 1 minute, until fragrant. Add the red wine and simmer until the liquid is reduced by just over half and starts to thicken. Remove from heat and let cool slightly; it can be lukewarm, but not hot for the next step.

In a separate bowl, incorporate the cooled reduction into the butter. Add the parsley and mix until well combined. Season with salt and pepper.

▪ ▪ ▪

Enjoy with steak or burgers fresh off the grill, potatoes, warm bread or scrambled eggs.

Goat's cheese butter

▪ ▪ ▪ SERVES 4 ▪ ▪ ▪

150 g (5½ oz) salted butter, softened
200 g (7 oz) soft goat's cheese

OPTIONAL FLAVOUR ADD-INS (CHOOSE ONE OR TWO)
1 tablespoon finely chopped thyme leaves or chives
1 teaspoon lemon zest
½ teaspoon crushed pink peppercorns
½ tablespoon granulated garlic
¼ teaspoon white wine vinegar

In a bowl, mix the butter until smooth – if you're using any add-ins, mix them with the butter until well combined. Add the goat's cheese, but don't over mix – leave some lumps and bumps for texture. Season with salt and pepper.

▪ ▪ ▪

Enjoy with a warm baguette or sourdough, potatoes, chicken or lamb fresh off the grill, roasted carrots, smoked salmon or scrambled eggs.

Sun-dried tomatoes, goat's cheese and pesto butter

▪ ▪ ▪ SERVES 4 ▪ ▪ ▪

150 g (5½ oz) salted butter, softened
2 tablespoons pesto
60 g (2 oz) goat's cheese, crumbled finely
2 tablespoons finely chopped sun-dried tomatoes

In a bowl, mix all the ingredients into the butter until well combined. Season with salt and pepper.

▪ ▪ ▪

Enjoy with steak fresh off the grill, pasta, potatoes, warm bread, crackers or scrambled eggs.

Brie, fig and caramelised onions butter

▪ ▪ ▪ SERVES 4 ▪ ▪ ▪

150 g (5½ oz) salted butter, softened
30 g (1 oz) brie, finely chopped and softened
¼ cup dried figs, finely chopped
½ cup caramelised onions
2 tablespoons finely chopped parsley

In a bowl, mix all the ingredients into the butter until well combined. Season to taste with salt and pepper.

▪ ▪ ▪

Enjoy with roasted chicken or pork, warm bread, crackers, your favourite vegetables, pasta or burgers fresh off the grill.

Tip

I use store-bought caramelised onions to make this recipe very simple. You can make your own caramelised onions by melting 2 tablespoons of unsalted butter in a frying pan over medium-high heat. Add 400 g (14 oz) sliced onions and a pinch of salt. Saute the onion for 5 minutes, stirring frequently. Reduce the heat to medium-low, then continue to cook for another 60-90 minutes, until the onion is sweet and golden brown.

Café de Paris butter

▪ ▪ ▪ SERVES 4 ▪ ▪ ▪

150 g (5½ oz) unsalted cultured butter, softened
1 small French shallot, finely chopped
2 teaspoons Dijon mustard
1 teaspoon finely chopped capers
2 anchovy fillets, finely chopped (optional)
1 teaspoon Worcestershire sauce
1 teaspoon lemon zest
1 teaspoon lemon juice
1 teaspoon tomato paste
1 teaspoon paprika
½ teaspoon curry powder
1 tablespoon finely chopped flat-leaf parsley
1 tablespoon finely chopped chives
½ teaspoon sea salt

In a bowl, use a hand-held mixer or spatula to beat the butter until light and creamy.

Mix in the remaining ingredients until well combined. Season with pepper.

▪ ▪ ▪

Enjoy with steak fresh off the grill, roasted chicken, grilled or pan-seared fish, your favourite vegetables, warm bread, fried or poached eggs, pasta or grains.

Tip

For extra depth, you can saute the shallot gently in a little butter before mixing it in.

'Nduja butter

▪ ▪ ▪ SERVES 4 ▪ ▪ ▪

150 g (5½ oz) salted butter, softened
40 g (1½ oz) 'nduja paste
1 clove garlic, finely grated
½ teaspoon lemon zest

In a bowl, mix all the ingredients into the butter until well combined.

▪ ▪ ▪

Enjoy with pasta, crusty bread, grilled or pan-seared fish, roasted or grilled chicken, potatoes, scrambled eggs or on toasties.

Anchovy butter

▪ ▪ ▪ SERVES 4 ▪ ▪ ▪

8 anchovy fillets
1 garlic clove, whole
150 g (5½ oz) unsalted butter, softened

Add the anchovy fillets and garlic to a small saucepan over medium heat and saute for 2–3 minutes, until the anchovies are beginning to dissolve and the garlic is just starting to brown.

Discard the garlic. In a bowl, mix the anchovies into the butter until well combined.

▪ ▪ ▪

Enjoy with steak fresh off the grill, roasted chicken, poached eggs, or on pizza or toast.

Cotija and lime butter

▪ ▪ ▪ SERVES 4 ▪ ▪ ▪

150 g (5½ oz) salted butter, softened
100 g (3 ½ oz) cotija cheese, crumbled
1 tablespoon finely chopped coriander (cilantro) leaves
zest and juice of 1 lime
1 teaspoon chipotle sauce or powder or chilli flakes
1 clove garlic, minced
¼ teaspoon sea salt flakes

In a bowl, stir together the butter, cotija, coriander, lime zest and juice, chipotle sauce, garlic and salt until well blended.

▪ ▪ ▪

Enjoy with corn or chicken fresh off the grill, prawns (shrimp), fish tacos, warm sourdough or flatbread, your favourite vegetables or on a roasted vegetable toastie.

Hot honey butter

▪ ▪ ▪ SERVES 4 ▪ ▪ ▪

150 g (5½ oz) salted butter, softened
1 tablespoon honey
1 small red chilli, very finely minced, or ½ teaspoon dried chilli flakes
½ teaspoon lemon juice or apple cider vinegar
pinch of sea salt flakes (optional)
½ teaspoon finely grated garlic or pinch of smoked paprika (optional)

In a bowl, beat the butter by hand until smooth and slightly fluffy. Add the honey and mix until well combined. Stir in the chilli, then add the lemon juice. Taste and adjust the flavours, adding the salt flakes and garlic if desired.

▪ ▪ ▪

Enjoy with corn on the cob, fried chicken, roasted pumpkin (winter squash), warm bread or crumpets.

BBQ butter from Banner Butter

▪ ▪ ▪ SERVES 4 ▪ ▪ ▪

150 g (5½ oz) salted cultured butter, softened
1 teaspoon smoked paprika
½ teaspoon garlic powder
½ teaspoon onion powder
½ teaspoon mild chilli powder
¼ teaspoon cayenne pepper (optional)
½ teaspoon salt
½ teaspoon ground black pepper
1 teaspoon brown sugar or maple sugar
1 teaspoon tomato paste (concentrated puree)
½ teaspoon Worcestershire sauce
¼ teaspoon apple cider vinegar

In a bowl, mix the spices and sugar. Stir in the tomato paste, Worcestershire sauce and apple cider vinegar. Add the butter and continue mixing until well combined.

▪ ▪ ▪

Enjoy with the crispy smashed potatoes from Banner Butter on page 122.

Miso butter

▪ ▪ ▪ SERVES 4 ▪ ▪ ▪

150 g (5½ oz) salted cultured butter, softened
100 g (3 ½ oz) white miso paste (or red miso for a stronger, saltier flavour)
½ teaspoon soy sauce
½ teaspoon grated ginger (optional)
½ teaspoon sesame oil (optional)

In a bowl, mix all the ingredients into the butter until well combined, ensuring the miso is evenly distributed.

▪ ▪ ▪

Enjoy with steak or fish fresh off the grill, roasted chicken, your favourite vegetables, warm sourdough, rice, pasta or mixed into mashed potatoes.

Amazake butter

▪ ▪ ▪ SERVES 4 ▪ ▪ ▪

150 g (5½ oz) cultured butter, softened
60–80 g (2–2¾ oz) amazake (look for thick, porridge-like options)

In a bowl, mix the butter until smooth and creamy. Add the amazake a spoonful at a time, mixing until fully incorporated and silky – add less for a firmer, richer butter, or more for a smoother, spreadable style. Season with salt.

▪ ▪ ▪

Enjoy with warm sourdough, roasted sweet potatoes or pumpkin (winter squash), crumpets, on a hot bowl of porridge or melted over grilled peaches or nectarines.

Tip

Amazake is a traditional Japanese drink made from fermented rice that can be found in most Asian grocery stores.

Vadouvan butter

▪ ▪ ▪ SERVES 4 ▪ ▪ ▪

150 g (5½ oz) salted butter, softened
1 tablespoon vadouvan curry blend
½ teaspoon lemon juice
1 small garlic clove, finely grated
1 tablespoon chopped coriander (cilantro) or parsley leaves (optional)

In a bowl, mix all the ingredients into the butter until well combined, ensuring the curry powder is evenly distributed. Season with salt.

▪ ▪ ▪

Enjoy with roasted chicken, prawns (shrimp), scallops, grilled or pan-seared white fish, roasted cauliflower, lentils or chickpeas (garbanzo beans), toasted sourdough or flatbread.

Truffle butter

▪ ▪ ▪ SERVES 4 ▪ ▪ ▪

1–2 teaspoons finely grated black truffle
pinch of sea salt
150 g (5½ oz) salted cultured butter, softened

In a bowl, mix 1 teaspoon of the truffle and the salt until well combined, ensuring the truffle is evenly distributed. Season with pepper and add more truffle, if desired.

▪ ▪ ▪

Enjoy with pasta, mixed into risotto or polenta, scrambled eggs or on steak fresh off the grill.

Tip

Freeze your truffle butter to preserve the truffle's delicate fragrance. When serving, add it to hot dishes like pasta or eggs just before they leave the pan to release the truffle's true, earthy aroma.

Too easy lemon butter

▪ ▪ ▪ SERVES 4 ▪ ▪ ▪

150 g (5½ oz) unsalted butter, softened
220 g (1 cup) white sugar
zest and juice of 1 lemon
2 eggs, beaten

In a saucepan, combine the butter, sugar, lemon juice, and beaten eggs. Place over low heat and stir continuously until the mixture thickens and is just about to boil. Be careful not to let it boil fully, as this can curdle the eggs.

▪ ▪ ▪

Enjoy with pancakes, ice cream or yoghurt, berries, in cakes or tarts, or on pavlova.

Maple and bacon butter

▪ ▪ ▪ SERVES 4 ▪ ▪ ▪

150 g (5½ oz) unsalted butter, softened
100 g (3½ oz) finely chopped bacon
1 tablespoon finely chopped garlic
1½ tablespoons maple syrup
1 tablespoon finely chopped chives
pinch of salt
pinch of pepper

In a saucepan over low heat, melt the butter. Add the bacon and fry until slightly crispy. Turn the heat off and add the garlic. Transfer to a glass bowl and leave to cool. Add the maple syrup, chives, salt and pepper, and mix lightly but well.

▪ ▪ ▪

Enjoy with warm croissants, cornbread, waffles, pancakes, French toast, vegetables such as brussels sprouts, or scrambled eggs.

Chocolate espresso butter

▪ ▪ ▪ SERVES 4 ▪ ▪ ▪

150 g (5½ oz) salted butter, softened
1 tablespoon Dutch (unsweetened) cocoa powder
1 teaspoon good-quality instant coffee powder
1½ tablespoons icing (confectioners') sugar
½ teaspoon vanilla extract
pinch of sea salt flakes

In a bowl, mix all the ingredients into the butter until well combined. Taste and adjust sweetness if needed.

▪ ▪ ▪

Enjoy with warm fruit toast, croissants, pancakes, banana bread, waffles or mixed into hot milk drinks.

Salted caramel butter

▪ ▪ ▪ SERVES 4 ▪ ▪ ▪

150 g (5½ oz) salted butter, softened, plus 2 tablespoons
3 tablespoons brown sugar
1 tablespoon cream (or 2 teaspoons buttermilk for tang)
½ teaspoon vanilla paste
½ teaspoon flaky sea salt, plus extra to taste

In a small saucepan over medium heat, melt the 2 tablespoons of butter and cook for 1–2 minutes, until golden with a nutty aroma.

Stir in the brown sugar and cream. Simmer for 1 minute until glossy, then remove from the heat allow to cool.

Meanwhile, in a bowl, beat the remaining butter by hand until fluffy. Pour in the caramel mixture, add the vanilla and salt, and whip until smooth. Add an extra pinch of salt, if desired — the butter should be gently salty.

▪ ▪ ▪

Enjoy with croissants, pancakes, waffles, brioche or warm fruit loaf with cream cheese.

Gingerbread butter

▪ ▪ ▪ SERVES 4 ▪ ▪ ▪

150 g (5½ oz) salted butter, softened
20 g (3/4 oz) brown sugar (or dark muscovado for a deeper flavour)
1 tablespoon honey or molasses
1 teaspoon ground ginger
½ teaspoon ground cinnamon
¼ teaspoon ground nutmeg
¼ teaspoon ground cloves
½ teaspoon vanilla extract

In a bowl, beat the butter by hand until smooth and slightly fluffy. Add the brown sugar and beat until fully incorporated, then mix in the honey.

Add the ginger, cinnamon, nutmeg and cloves, then stir in the vanilla, mixing until evenly combined. Season with salt, if desired.

Let the butter rest for a few hours or overnight so the spices bloom.

▪ ▪ ▪

Enjoy with warm sourdough or fruit loaf, pancakes, waffles, crumpets or banana bread.

Cranberry, orange and dark chocolate butter

▪ ▪ ▪ SERVES 4 ▪ ▪ ▪

150 g (5½ oz) unsalted butter, softened
20 g (¾ oz) dried cranberries, finely chopped
½ teaspoon finely grated orange zest
1 teaspoon orange juice
2 teaspoon honey or maple syrup
15 g (½ oz) dark chocolate (70%), shaved or very finely chopped
pinch of flaky sea salt (optional)

In a bowl, beat the butter by hand until smooth and slightly fluffy. Add the cranberries, orange zest and juice, and honey, mixing until well combined. Fold in the chocolate and taste, adjusting the sweetness or citrus as desired,

Let the butter rest for a few hours or overnight so the orange and cranberry flavours bloom.

▪ ▪ ▪

Enjoy with warm fruit toast, brioche, crumpets, toasted sourdough, scones, panettone, croissants, on a hot bowl of porridge or baked oats, roasted sweet potato or pumpkin (winter squash).

Variation

Substitute the chocolate with 20 g (¾ oz) pistachios, lightly toasted and finely chopped.

Eggnog butter

▪ ▪ ▪ SERVES 4 ▪ ▪ ▪

150 g (5½ oz) salted butter, softened
1 tablespoon honey or maple syrup
½ teaspoon vanilla extract
¼ teaspoon freshly grated nutmeg
pinch of cinnamon
1–2 teaspoons dark rum or brandy (optional)

In a bowl, beat the butter by hand until smooth and slightly fluffy. Add the remaining ingredients, mixing until well combined. Taste and adjust the sweetness or spice if needed.

Let the butter rest for a few hours or overnight so the spices bloom.

▪ ▪ ▪

Enjoy with warm brioche, fruit toast, panettone, pancakes, waffles, French toast, a hot bowl of porridge, or baked apples.

Some other flavours to consider…

Parmesan and cracked pepper; horseradish and chives; capers, mustard and chives; nori; lemon and miso; saffron and dates; smoked paprika; pesto; za'atar; thyme, rosemary and garlic; blue cheese; pumpkin spice; vanilla and cardamon/cinnamon; or cinnamon and maple.

Butter boards revisited

The mere mention of a butter board makes me recoil. Smearing butter directly onto a board for everyone to dip - and inevitably double-dip - into with bread, knives, tongs or whatever happens to be closest feels less like serving and more like an abuse of the ingredient. Add a warm room to the mix and what begins as a spectacle might quickly have you donning a hazmat suit and running for the door!

If the impulse behind butter boards is to treat butter with the same care we give cheese, there is a far better way to do it. Serving butter in small ramekins or dishes allows each style to remain distinct, clean and properly tempered. Different butters can then be paired thoughtfully with bread, crackers, vegetables, dried fruit or nuts, inviting tasting rather than excess. Presented this way, butter becomes something to engage with deliberately - shared, yes, but respected.

Once butter is treated with this level of care, it naturally opens the door to using flavoured butters more deliberately. Rather than acting as decoration or novelty, they can take the place of dips altogether. Butter carries flavour efficiently, meaning a small amount goes a long way, seasoning food without the heaviness of oil-based spreads or emulsions. Served cool but pliable, flavoured butter invites dipping, dragging and tasting while remaining composed and controlled.

SERVING FLAVOURED BUTTERS AS A SHARED PLATTER

Prepare a small selection of your favourite flavoured butters in advance, keeping the flavours distinct and purposeful (refer to pages 74–89 of this book for recipes and guidance). Spoon each butter into its own ramekin or small bowl and allow them to soften slightly at room temperature until pliable but still holding their shape. This is important — butter that is too cold is difficult to use, and butter that is too warm quickly loses its appeal.

Serve the ramekins with their own butter knife, alongside a considered mix of accompaniments: good bread, crackers, raw or lightly blanched vegetables, dried fruit, nuts or anything else that welcomes richness. Keep the offering generous but not excessive. Butter works best when it is invited, not overwhelmed.

As well, consider acidic additions such as pickles, cornichons or capers. The reason is simple: fat coats the mouth and can dull flavour, while a little acidity cuts through that richness and refreshes the palate. That's why pickles appear so often on cheese boards and charcuterie platters; they're not just there for colour or decoration, but serve a practical purpose, bringing balance and brightness to each bite.

Serve with small forks and butter knives and encourage guests to help themselves. This approach works particularly well for a relaxed brunch or an afternoon tête-à-tête, where people can dip, drag and taste at their own pace. Presented this way, flavoured butter becomes both practical and social — shared, deliberate and treated with the respect it deserves.

FLAVOURED BUTTER PAIRINGS

. . .

HERB AND GARLIC BUTTER (PAGE 76)
Works well with blanched or grilled vegetables, radishes, boiled eggs, pickled onions and crusty bread.

HOT HONEY BUTTER (PAGE 83)
Works well with toasted sourdough, warm flatbread, charred ciabatta, grilled halloumi, crispy bacon and a selection of roasted nuts.

MISO BUTTER (PAGE 84)
Works well with cucumber, roasted squash, rice crackers or simple grains. Umami replaces acidity, adding depth without heaviness.

ANCHOVY BUTTER (PAGE 82)
Works well with warm focaccia, crostini, pickled shallots, green olives and lightly cooked seafood, where salinity sharpens richness.

CAFÉ DE PARIS BUTTER (PAGE 81)
Works well with grilled sourdough, warm focaccia, pickled carrots, capers, roasted peppers and prosciutto or salami.

GINGERBREAD BUTTER (PAGE 88)
Works well with toasted fruit scones, dried fruit crackers, lightly toasted panettone, pickled cherries, dried fig halves and a selection of roasted nuts.

LAGUIOLE

BUTTER IN

THE KITCHEN

SNACKS AND DRINKS

Cultured butter bullet coffee

It did cross my mind to rename this drink 'Lard Ass kick ass coffee' because it is such an energising drink, perfect for mornings when you want something to nourish, comfort and power you through the day. The cultured butter offers a rich flavour and velvety texture. It's simple, satisfying and gloriously buttery.

▪ ▪ ▪ SERVES 1 ▪ ▪ ▪

250 ml (1 cup) freshly brewed strong coffee
1 tablespoon unsalted cultured butter
splash of warm milk or steamed milk (optional)

Put the hot coffee and butter in a blender and mix for 10–15 seconds until creamy and frothy. The blender is essential here – it creates that silky latte texture and prevents separation. Pour into your favourite mug and add the warm milk, if desired.

Variations

Chocolate latte bullet: Add 1 tablespoon Chocolate espresso butter (page 87) instead of the unsalted butter.

Mocha latte bullet: Add 1 teaspoon cacao powder.

Vanilla latte bullet: Add 1 teaspoon vanilla extract.

Spiced latte bullet: Add a pinch of cinnamon and a pinch of nutmeg.

Cultured buttermilk smoothie

Cultured buttermilk is naturally high in protein, light in fat and, due to its lactic acid, good for the gut microbiome. It blends into a creamy, refreshing smoothie base without the heaviness of yoghurt or milk, making it a perfect everyday protein drink.

This recipe is for my smoothie base, ready to riff off whatever fruit or other bits you have handy. For a thicker smoothie, use frozen banana or add 2 tablespoons of oats and let them soften for 5 minutes before blending.

▪ ▪ ▪ SERVES 1 ▪ ▪ ▪

250 ml (1 cup) cultured buttermilk (see Tip on page 106)
1 ripe banana (fresh or frozen)
1 large handful of ice
1–2 tablespoons honey or maple syrup
½ teaspoon vanilla extract (optional)
pinch of salt

Mix all the ingredients in a blender until smooth and frothy. Taste and adjust sweetness or thickness as needed. Pour into a chilled glass and drink immediately.

Best enjoyed right away, but you can refrigerate the smoothie up to 24 hours and re-blend before serving.

Variations

Make the base, above, and add any of the following...

Green glow: 1 handful of baby spinach, ½ avocado and 1 tablespoon chia seeds

Berry burst: 130 g (1 cup) mixed berries (fresh or frozen) and the zest of ½ lemon

Tropical morning: 160 g (½ cup) chopped mango, 80 g (½ cup) chopped pineapple and a squeeze of lime juice

Spiced date and cinnamon: 3 pitted dates, ¼ teaspoon cinnamon and a small pinch of nutmeg

Coffee pick-me-up: 3 tablespoons cold-brew coffee, 1 teaspoon cacao powder and a dash of maple syrup

Strawberry sweetness: 90 g (1 cup) chopped strawberries, 2 teaspoons honey, 1 tablespoon oats and a squeeze of lemon juice

Ghee-roasted nuts

This is the recipe I turn to whenever I find a left-over packet of nuts hidden in the back of the pantry. Sprinkle these over salads or serve on a grazing board alongside drinks. You can even turn them into gifts by filling glass jars and tying a ribbon around the lid – perfect for Christmas.

▪ ▪ ▪ SERVES 6 ▪ ▪ ▪

420 g (3 cups) mixed nuts (almonds, cashews, pecans, walnuts, macadamias)
3 tablespoons ghee, melted
1½ teaspoons sea salt
1 teaspoon smoked paprika (optional)
½ teaspoon garlic powder or cumin (optional)

Preheat the oven to 150°C (300°F) fan-forced and line an oven tray with baking paper.

Toss the nuts in the melted ghee, salt and spices, if using. Spread evenly over the tray and roast for 12–15 minutes, stirring once, until golden and fragrant.

Leave to cool completely – the nuts will crisp up as they cool.

Store the nuts in an airtight container at room temperature for 2–3 weeks, or in the fridge for 4–6 weeks, and up to 3 months in the freezer.

Variations

Ghee candied nuts: Leave out the paprika and garlic powder. Instead, mix the ghee with 3 tablespoons maple syrup or honey, 1 teaspoon cinnamon and a pinch of sea salt. Coat the nuts and roast for 15 minutes, watching carefully that they don't burn. The nuts will be glossy and slightly sticky, and you can sprinkle with extra salt flakes while still warm, if you enjoy that salty–sweet crunch.

Spiced chilli ghee nuts: Leave out the paprika and garlic powder. Instead, mix the ghee with 1 teaspoon chilli flakes, ½ teaspoon ground cumin, ½ teaspoon smoked paprika and 1 teaspoon sea salt for a warm, punchy finish.

Herb and parmesan ghee nuts: Use just cashews and almonds here. Leave out the paprika and garlic powder. Instead, mix the ghee with 1 teaspoon dried rosemary or thyme, 1 teaspoon sea salt and 50 g (½ cup) finely grated parmesan. Sprinkle with more parmesan while hot, then leave to cool before serving.

Spicy roasted chickpeas

These are very easy and make a great salad topper or healthy snack, although it's impossible to stop at just one handful! Their golden crunch and nutty depth comes from being roasted in ghee rather than the heavier olive oil.

▪ ▪ ▪ SERVES 4 ▪ ▪ ▪

2 teaspoons ghee
400 g (14 oz) tinned chickpeas (garbanzo beans), rinsed
¾ teaspoon sea salt
½ teaspoon ground black pepper
1 teaspoon dried oregano
¼ teaspoon cayenne pepper or smoked paprika

Preheat the oven to 200°C (400°F) fan-forced.

Spoon the ghee into a roasting tin and warm in the oven for 1–2 minutes until melted.

Drain and pat the chickpeas dry with paper towel and discard any loose skins. Add the salt, pepper, oregano and cayenne to the ghee in the bottom of the tin and stir well. Add the chickpeas and shake to coat them in the spiced oil.

Roast for 30–35 minutes, or until golden-brown and crunchy, shaking the tin regularly to prevent the chickpeas sticking. Cool before serving.

Store the roasted chickpeas for 3–5 days in an airtight container at room temperature; they start to soften after about 5 days. They will keep for 1 week in the fridge and up to 1 month in the freezer.

Buttermilk crackers

These crackers owe their tender crunch and delicate flakiness to the buttermilk. It encourages light layers to form and helps achieve a crisp finish. Just take care not to overwork the dough or you'll end up with something closer to bathroom tiles!

▪ ▪ ▪ MAKES 24 ▪ ▪ ▪

300 g (2 cups) plain (all-purpose) flour
2 teaspoons baking powder
1 teaspoon sea salt flakes, plus extra for sprinkling
120 g (4½ oz) unsalted cultured butter, plus extra to serve (optional)
125 ml (½ cup) cultured buttermilk (see Tip)
dip or cheese of your choice, to serve (optional)
creamed honey, to serve (optional)

Combine the flour, baking powder and salt in a food processor. Cut the butter into 8 pieces and add it to the processor. Pulse until the mixture looks like fine breadcrumbs.

With the processor running, pour in the buttermilk and process just until the dough comes together in a ball. Flatten into a disc, wrap in plastic wrap and refrigerate for at least an hour.

Preheat the oven to 160°C (320°F) fan-forced and line a large baking tray with baking paper.

Pull off a third of the dough and leave the remainder in the fridge. Roll out the dough thinly, about 3 mm (¼ in) thick. Sprinkle lightly with more salt and poke all over with a fork.

Using the tip of a sharp knife or a biscuit cutter or glass, cut the dough into circles, squares, diamonds or any shape you like. Transfer to the baking tray with a spatula.

Bake for 10–15 minutes, or until just turning golden. Cool completely on a rack.

Serve with your choice of accompaniments, such as hummus, cheese, or butter and creamed honey. You can also serve the crackers on a butter board.

Store the crackers in an airtight container for up to 3 weeks.

Tip

If you can't find cultured buttermilk, make your own by adding ½ tablespoon lemon juice to 125 ml (½ cup) milk, then leave at room temperature for 30 minutes.

Cultured buttermilk ranch dip with veggie sticks

Fresh, creamy, herby and tangy – this ranch dressing leans into real cultured dairy for depth and balance. As well as using it as a dip, you can drizzle it over crunchy salads or avocado toast, spoon it over roast potatoes or fried chicken, or serve it with prawns or grilled fish. Once you've made ranch like this, there's no going back to store-bought dressing.

▪ ▪ ▪ SERVES 6–8 ▪ ▪ ▪

125 ml (½ cup) cultured buttermilk (see Tip on page 106)
125 ml (½ cup) sour cream or crème fraîche
125 ml (½ cup) mayonnaise
1 small garlic clove, finely grated (or ½ teaspoon garlic powder)
1 teaspoon Dijon mustard
1 tablespoon lemon juice or white wine vinegar
1 teaspoon onion powder
1 tablespoon finely chopped chives
1 tablespoon finely chopped parsley
½ tablespoon finely chopped dill

Whisk together the buttermilk, sour cream and mayonnaise until smooth. Stir in the garlic, mustard, lemon juice, onion powder and fresh herbs. Season generously with salt and pepper. Refrigerate for at least 30 minutes for the flavours to develop before serving. If thicker than you'd like, thin with a splash more buttermilk.

Store the dip in a sealed jar in the fridge for up to 5 days.

The perfect butter toastie

There's something deeply satisfying about a good toastie, also known as a grilled cheese — biting into that golden, buttery crunch that gives way to soft, molten cheese that stretches from toast to teeth. The secret to a fabulous toastie is, without argument, the butter. For something extra, compound butters are next level and turn a simple toastie into something extraordinary, infusing flavour right into the bread as it crisps.

▪ ▪ ▪ SERVES 1 ▪ ▪ ▪

2–3 teaspoons compound butter of your choice (pages 74–89) or salted butter, softened, plus extra to finish
2 slices good-quality bread (sourdough, rye or chunky white)
50–100 g (1¾–3½ oz) freshly grated vintage cheddar, gruyere or mozzarella (or a blend of all three), depending on the size of your bread and desired cheesiness

Spread the compound butter evenly on one side of each bread slice; this will be the outside of your toastie. If desired, butter the inside of both slices for an extra buttery crunch.

Place the cheese on the non-buttered side of one slice of bread, then cover with the second slice, butter side up, and press lightly to hold together.

Heat a non-stick frying pan over medium heat or heat a sandwich press. Cook the toastie for 2–3 minutes per side, using a spatula to press down gently if cooking in a pan, until golden and crisp.

Slice in half and serve warm – ideally with a little extra melted butter brushed over the top.

FLAVOURED BUTTER AND TOASTIE PAIRINGS

To make your toasties even more delicious, try adding extra fillings and experimenting with different cheeses. Below is a list of some possibilities, using this book's compound butters recipes.

. . .

HERB & GARLIC BUTTER (PAGE 76)
- Mozzarella, vintage cheddar, tomato and basil

BBQ BUTTER (PAGE 84)
- Shredded roast chicken and three-cheese blend of mozzarella, vintage cheddar and parmesan

TRUFFLE BUTTER (PAGE 86)
- Taleggio or provolone, sliced Swiss brown mushrooms and a pinch of salt flakes

HOT HONEY BUTTER (PAGE 83)
- Thinly sliced mortadella ham and buffalo mozzarella

MISO BUTTER (PAGE 84)
- Gouda/gruyere and mild cheddar, kimchi and a pinch of minced garlic

BRIE, FIG AND CARAMELISED ONIONS BUTTER (PAGE 81)
- Thinly sliced ham and sliced brie

GARLIC BUTTER (PAGE 76)
- Sliced baguette, thinly sliced smoked leg ham, gruyere and chopped parsley

ANCHOVY BUTTER (PAGE 82)
- Sourdough bread and unsalted butter (or salted to make it extra salty)

ROSEMARY BUTTER (PAGE 77)
- Sliced baguette and grilled flank steak or minute steak

GINGERBREAD BUTTER (PAGE 88)
- Fruit loaf, ricotta or mascarpone, mashed banana and honey

VEGETABLES

Roasted vadouvan cauliflower

This recipe is thanks to food writer and reviewer Jill Dupleix, whose mother, Rosemary, I know better than Jill herself. Rosemary was one of my first customers when I began making butter and selling it at Ocean Grove Farmers' Market. Like my family, Rosemary's is from south-west Victoria, one of Australia's largest dairy regions.

▪ ▪ ▪ SERVES 4 ▪ ▪ ▪

1 cauliflower, cut into florets
2 tablespoons olive oil
1 tablespoon salted butter
2 teaspoons vadouvan curry powder
2 tablespoons chopped parsley leaves

Heat the oven to 180°C (350°F) fan-forced.

Toss the cauliflower in the olive oil. Scatter over a baking tray and bake for 40 minutes or until golden and tender. Season well with salt and pepper.

Melt the butter in a non-stick frying pan over low heat and stir in the vadouvan powder. Add the cauliflower and toss for a minute or two until well coated (don't let it burn). Scatter with the parsley and serve hot.

Beurre blanc for vegetables

Beurre blanc is a classic French butter sauce and is kitchen magic, in my opinion: simple, versatile and able to make almost anything look and taste better with very little effort. It smooths, brightens and brings everything together, which is why I think of it as my essential sauce. It's excellent over asparagus, green beans, baby carrots or potatoes. It's also great with seafood such as snapper, flathead, barramundi, salmon or trout, or even over left-over roast chicken.

▪ ▪ ▪ SERVES 2 ▪ ▪ ▪

3 French shallots, finely diced
60 ml (¼ cup) dry white wine
60 ml (¼ cup) white wine vinegar
225 g (8 oz) unsalted butter, chilled and diced
your favourite steamed vegetables, to serve

Mix the shallot, wine and vinegar in a small saucepan over low heat. Bring to the boil, then reduce to a gentle simmer. Simmer for 7–10 minutes, stirring occasionally as the liquids reduce and the flavours combine. Remove from the heat when the liquid has reduced to a syrup.

Allow the pan to cool, then return to low heat and start adding the cold butter. Add a single cube at a time, whisking in each one until it has fully melted before the next cube is added.

If the sauce splits during this process, remove from the heat and whisk in 1 teaspoon cold water to bring it back together. Continue until the last cube of butter has melted. Remove from the heat and keep whisking for another 10–15 seconds. If the sauce is too thin, place back on the heat and whisk for another 10–20 seconds.

Season with salt and white pepper. Strain if you prefer a smooth sauce, or leave the shallots in for texture. Check the flavour and add a squeeze of lemon or a splash more vinegar for brightness, if needed. Serve immediately over vegetables.

Beurre blanc is best served immediately, but, if needed, can be kept it in an airtight container in the fridge for up to 24 hours. Reheat very gently over a warm water bath, whisking constantly to re-emulsify. Avoid boiling or microwaving, as the sauce will split. Beurre blanc does not freeze well.

Variations

Brown beurre blanc: Replace half of the butter with browned butter (see page 138).

Herb beurre blanc: Stir in a few teaspoons of chopped chives, parsley, dill or tarragon at the end.

Citrus beurre blanc: Add 1 teaspoon finely grated lemon or orange zest.

Caper beurre blanc: Fold in 1 teaspoon chopped capers.

BANNER
UNSALTED
BUTTER
BANNER BUTTER
BANNER
SEA SALT
BUTTER

ANDREW MCBATH

Banner Butter

ATLANTA, USA

...

SMALL, SIMPLE, SLOW

When we speak, Andrew McBath is relaxed, thoughtful and very clear about one thing in particular: Banner Butter was never meant to be fast food.

He started the business in 2012 in Georgia, a 'dairy-deficit state' where good cream is surprisingly hard to come by. Andrew didn't grow up in a creamery; his reference point was his grandfather, who worked for Coca-Cola, and the idea of a beautiful, honest product on a shelf that people would seek out again and again. Butter, as it turned out, was the thing that captured his imagination.

Andrew and his wife began with compound butters, playing with flavours at home. But local chefs kept asking for something more basic yet more radical: a genuinely local butter, salted and unsalted, made with care. That sent Andrew down a rabbit hole – reading old dairy journals, learning about culturing and fermentation, visiting Brittany and its wall of farmhouse butters, and talking to makers in Ireland, the UK and Australia.

Today, every Banner product begins as cultured butter. The flavoured butters – BBQ; honey habanero; berbere; cinnamon, cardamom & ginger; roasted garlic & basil; blue cheese, sea salt & cracked pepper; dark chocolate and many more – are expressions on top of that, rather than a substitute for it. Each is handcrafted in small batches and wrapped in rustic parchment, making them as beautiful as they are delicious. Banner Butter has become a darling of farmers' markets, artisanal food shops and chefs, offering Americans a butter experience that feels both rooted in tradition and refreshingly modern.

Andrew describes Banner's philosophy as small, simple, slow. They automate what makes sense, but the heart of the work stays human: watching the churn, deciding when to stop, staying connected to processors and farmers in a system that rarely rewards slowness. Banner Butter lives in that tension – large enough to grow, but small enough to still care about every single batch.

Crispy smashed potatoes from Banner Butter

This recipe comes from Drew and his brilliant team at Banner Butter in Atlanta, Georgia. They consistently do fabulous things with flavoured butter, pushing ideas while keeping a sense of play and joy at the centre of everything they create. This recipe uses Banner Butter's smoked sea salt butter. If you're in the US and can get your hands on it, I highly recommend doing so. If not, liquid smoke (available at barbecue stores and some supermarkets) is a simple workaround that still delivers all the flavour.

▪ ▪ ▪ SERVES 4 ▪ ▪ ▪

500 g (1 lb 2 oz) fingerling potatoes (kipfler or similar), unpeeled
1 tablespoon sea salt, plus extra for sprinkling
85 g (3 oz) unsalted butter, at room temperature
2–4 drops liquid smoke (mesquite or hickory; see Tip)
2 tablespoons extra virgin olive oil
3 red chillies, thinly sliced (optional)

Place the potatoes in a saucepan and cover generously with cold water. Add the salt, then bring to the boil and cook for about 20 minutes, until tender.

Meanwhile, place the butter in a small bowl and mix in the liquid smoke. Set aside.

Drain the potatoes. Place on a chopping board, cover with a clean cloth and gently press down with your palm to smash the potatoes to about 1 cm (½ in) thick. Leave to cool completely, then transfer to a paper-lined baking tray.

Preheat the oven to 210°C (410°F) fan-forced.

Melt the smoked butter in a small pan over low heat. Measure out the butter and add enough olive oil to give you a total of 3 tablespoons.

Drizzle the butter and oil mixture over the potatoes, gently moving them around to ensure they are evenly coated. Sprinkle with salt to taste. Bake for 15 minutes. Remove from the oven and turn over. Add the chillies, if desired, and bake for another 15–20 minutes, until golden brown and crispy.

Tip

If using smoked Banner Butter, simply skip the liquid smoke.

Potato rosti with feta, avocado and salsa

Cooking potatoes in ghee is a game changer. Ghee's high smoke point means the potatoes fry to a golden crisp without burning, while its nutty, caramel flavour seeps into every bite. The inside of this rosti is fluffy and buttery, while the outside audibly crunches. Olive oil just doesn't give the same depth of flavour and crispiness.

▪ ▪ ▪ SERVES 4 ▪ ▪ ▪

- 150 g (5½ oz) cherry tomatoes, quartered
- 1 French shallot, finely diced
- 1 kg (2 lb 3 oz) sebago potatoes
- 80 ml (⅓ cup) ghee, melted
- 4 eggs
- avocado, quartered
- 30 g (½ cup) chopped dill
- 30 g (½ cup) mint leaves
- 15 g (¼ cup) chopped chives
- 2 tablespoons capers, rinsed and chopped
- 100 g (3½ oz) feta, crumbled

In a bowl, combine the tomato and shallot. Set aside.

Peel the potatoes and cut into matchsticks with a mandolin, or coarsely grate. Squeeze out as much liquid as possible, then transfer to a large bowl. Add 2 tablespoons of the ghee, season well with salt and pepper and toss to coat evenly.

Heat a 30 cm (12 in) non-stick frying pan over medium heat. Add 1 tablespoon of the remaining ghee and swirl to coat the base. Gently scatter the potato into the pan, spreading evenly, but without pressing down. You want a crisp crust with a soft interior. Cook for 15 minutes or until the underside is golden and crisp.

Place a large plate over the pan and carefully invert the rosti onto it, then slide it back into the pan. Add the remaining 1 tablespoon ghee around the edge and cook for another 10 minutes, or until the underside is golden and crisp.

While the rosti is cooking, heat another large frying pan over medium heat. Crack the eggs into the pan and fry to your liking.

Transfer the rosti to a board and cut into four wedges. Top with the tomato and shallot mixture and the avacado. Scatter with the herbs, capers and feta, and serve each wedge with a fried egg.

Perfectly crisp ghee-roasted potatoes

Crispy roast potatoes are a benchmark in our home. Mike, my husband, is always on a mission to make the crunchiest potatoes; he is British, after all! He has used every potato known to man – parboiled, not parboiled, salted, not salted, high heat, low heat, olive oil, butter, a mix of the two – until I turned his attention to ghee. I feel he can now rest, knowing he has found the ultimate recipe.

▪ ▪ ▪ SERVES 4 ▪ ▪ ▪

1 kg (2 lb 3 oz) brushed potatoes, scrubbed but unpeeled, chopped into 2 cm (¾ in) cubes
120 g (4½ oz) ghee

Place the potato in a saucepan and cover generously with cold water. Add a good pinch of salt and bring to the boil. Cook for 10–15 minutes until tender.

Preheat the oven to 200°C (400°F) fan-forced.

Drain the potato, giving the colander a good shake so the chunks are roughed up and messy. Place the ghee in a roasting tin and melt in the hot oven for 1–2 minutes.

Tip the potato into the hot roasting tin, tossing so the pieces are coated with the ghee.

Roast for 50–60 minutes until crisp and golden, tossing every 20 minutes so they are roasted evenly. Sprinkle with sea salt and serve immediately.

Pumpkinkopita with burnt butter sage

This recipe is by Slow Food Melbourne, with thanks to their president, Alison Peake. Slow Food believes food should be 'good, clean and fair', and that means focusing on local seasonal produce. There is nothing more local than homegrown, so think about growing pumpkins in your garden and using fresh butter to make this pastry. Try growing your own herbs, such as sage, so you always have them on hand.

▪ ▪ ▪ SERVES 8 ▪ ▪ ▪

500–600 g (about 1 lb 3 oz) pumpkin (winter squash), peeled and diced
120 g (4½ oz) salted butter, melted
10 sheets filo pastry
100 g (3½ oz) feta

BURNT BUTTER TOPPING
50 g (1¾ oz) salted butter
2 tablespoons finely chopped sage leaves
20 g (¾ oz) hazelnuts, walnuts or other nuts, roughly chopped

Preheat the oven to 180°C (350°F) fan-forced.

Scatter the pumpkin on a baking tray and brush with about 2 tablespoons of the melted butter. Bake for 30 minutes. Mash the pumpkin or leave it diced and measure out 2 cups.

Meanwhile, line a baking tray with baking paper. Lay one sheet of filo on the tray and brush with the melted butter. Put another sheet on top and brush with butter. Keep layering filo sheets and brushing with butter until you've used all of the sheets.

Roll the edges of the pastry up to create a pie shell and brush the edges with melted butter.

Evenly distribute the pumpkin in the pie shell. Crumble the feta over the pumpkin, then bake for 30–35 minutes, until the pastry is lightly brown on the edges.

When the pumpkinkopita is cooked, make the burnt butter topping. Melt the butter in a small saucepan over medium heat until bubbling and starting to change colour. Add the sage leaves and cook for 1 minute, then pour the burnt butter over the pumpkin and feta. Finish with the chopped nuts and serve.

Mashed potatoes Robuchon-style

No one championed mashed potatoes quite like Joël Robuchon, the Michelin-starred 'chef of the century'. His 'two parts potato to one part butter' ratio is iconic. In one famous kitchen clip, he urges his cooks with a flourish: 'Encore du beurre, du beurre, du beurre!' More butter, more butter, more butter! It's indulgence at its finest, and it transforms simple mash into something unforgettable. If you are unable to get your hands on ratte potatoes, use a variety that is waxy so it holds its structure and can absorb the butter.

▪ ▪ ▪ SERVES 6 ▪ ▪ ▪

1 kg (2 lb 3 oz) potatoes, preferably rattes, unpeeled
250 g (9 oz) unsalted cultured butter, chilled and diced
250 ml (1 cup) full-cream (whole) milk, warmed

Add the potatoes to a large saucepan and cover generously with cold water. Add a good pinch of salt and bring to the boil. Reduce to a simmer and cook for about 20–30 minutes until tender. Drain the potatoes and place in a container with a tea towel on top to keep them warm.

Peel the potatoes while they're hot and place in a second container that's covered with plastic wrap on top with a slit in the centre for you to drop your peeled potatoes through, again to maintain their heat.

Pass the potatoes through a potato ricer into a saucepan. Place over medium heat to warm the potato and stir for 3–5 minutes to evaporate off any moisture.

Pass the potato through a fine-mesh sieve, pushing with the back of a serving spoon – this will break down the potato to give a much finer consistency and prevent it getting gummy or overworked.

Put the potato back into a pan over medium heat and gradually incorporate the cold cubes of butter, stirring slowly and methodically while adding the butter to ensure an emulsion-like consistency. Add the warmed milk a bit at a time (warming the milk prevents it 'shocking' the potato), stirring constantly so as not to break the emulsion, until the potato has a creamy, fluffy consistency.

Season with sea salt, to taste, and perhaps a pinch of white pepper.

Roasted asparagus and leeks with burnt butter almond crunch

My life turned around the day I realised leeks and asparagus were a perfect match — and burnt butter was the wedding ring. I never thought asparagus could be this exciting, but this combo proved me wrong. Simple, bold and unbelievably good. Add ½ teaspoon chilli flakes to the burnt butter for extra punch, if you like.

▪ ▪ ▪ SERVES 2–4 ▪ ▪ ▪

2 large leeks
600 g (1 lb 5 oz) asparagus (about 2 bunches)
1 tablespoon extra virgin olive oil
30 g (⅓ cup) flaked almonds
90 g (⅓ cup) salted cultured butter
10 g (½ cup) mint leaves

Preheat the oven to 200°C (400°F) fan-forced and line a baking tray with baking paper.

Cut the leeks into 2 cm (¾ in) rounds and the asparagus into halves or thirds, then place on the tray. Coat with the olive oil and season generously with salt and pepper.

Roast in the oven for 15 minutes or until the vegetables are soft and slightly charred, turning once.

To make burnt butter toasted almonds, heat a small non-stick frying pan over high heat. Add the almonds and toast until just golden. Reduce the heat to medium and add the butter. Cook the butter briefly for 1 minute until it begins to bubble and turn golden brown, then turn off the heat.

Arrange the roasted vegetables on a serving platter and top with the hot buttery almonds. Finish with a scattering of mint and serve immediately.

MARIA VAN ZYL

Cream of the Crop Micro Dairy

PIKET-BO-BERG, SOUTH AFRICA

...

BUTTER FROM THE HIGH SLOPES OF THE SWARTLAND

When we speak, Maria Van Zyl has been up since dawn, milking cows on the windswept slopes of the Swartland in South Africa. Her micro dairy, Cream of the Crop, sits high in the hills where apple and pear orchards dominate and small dairies have mostly disappeared. Her tiny herd of Brown Swiss cows – and the butter she makes from them – feels like a quiet refusal to let this kind of farming fade away. Cream of the Crop is a biodynamic micro-dairy founded on principles of craftsmanship, sustainability and connection to the land.

Maria's love of dairy began in Italy, where she studied with Slow Food at Italy's University of Gastronomic Sciences near Bra in Piedmont. She learnt to read milk the way some people read wine. She returned home determined to bring authenticity to South African dairy but struggled to make cheese given the lack of fresh, local milk that was available. Then she tasted cultured butter at a friend's pop-up diner. South Africa had none – so she decided to change that.

She started in her mother's kitchen, selling at markets and later producing weekly food boxes that boomed during the pandemic. Eventually her family moved to the farm, where she now crafts cultured butter using a traditional fermentation method with kefir grains – fermenting fresh warm milk into a mild kefir gel and blending it into cream before a gentle churn for buttery texture and tang.

The result is butter with a bright, elegant acidity – something between a Granny Smith apple and a young Chardonnay – salted with coarse sea salt that gives a light crunch.

Workshops at the farm reconnect visitors to cows, milk and real food. Maria knows her butter is expensive in an industrial-price world, but she won't compromise. She wants people to taste it and feel, just for a moment, that they've never *truly* tasted butter before.

PASTA, RICE AND GRAINS

Pasta with brown butter

Brown butter is what happens when patience and heat turn ordinary butter into something extraordinary. If you've ever walked into a kitchen where butter has just hit a hot pan, you'll know the magic of that aroma – nutty, toasty, with hints of caramel and roasted hazelnuts.

Brown butter turns simple dishes into something memorable. Swirled through pasta, drizzled over vegetables or whisked into mashed potatoes, it makes everything a little more indulgent. When browning, be sure to start with a clean, bright stainless-steel pan for ease of colour identification – a non-stick pan is no friend of brown butter.

▪ ▪ ▪ SERVES 4 ▪ ▪ ▪

300 g (11 oz) spaghetti, linguine, gnocchi or ravioli
110 g (4 oz) unsalted butter
100 g (1 cup) grated parmesan, plus extra to serve

Bring a large pan of generously salted water to the boil. Add the pasta and cook until al dente, following the packet directions. Drain, keeping 125 ml (½ cup) of the pasta water.

Melt the butter over medium–low heat in a wide frying pan (don't use non-stick) or a flameproof casserole dish (Dutch oven; a light-coloured base will help you see the colour change).

The water in the butter needs to cook off so that the temperature of the butter can rise above 100°C (210°F). When the butter stops bubbling, reduce the heat to low.

Cook for 3–4 minutes, swirling the pan occasionally as the butter foams while the milk solids turn golden brown and release a nutty aroma – watch the butter closely. Remove from the heat immediately to prevent burning.

Add the pasta to the brown butter and toss to coat. Stir in the parmesan until it melts, then stir in a little of the pasta water, a tablespoon at a time, until the sauce clings and looks silky. Finish with extra parmesan and pepper.

Variation:

Add 8–10 sage leaves to the brown butter before taking it off the heat.

Spaghetti with lemon and anchovies

My mum was a fabulous cook who taught herself to create beautiful meals on our dairy farm to feed a large family of eight. She collected recipes wherever she found them and kept them in a biscuit tin – many torn from magazines in doctors' waiting rooms or hairdressers. This classic recipe was one of her finds.

▪ ▪ ▪ SERVES 4 ▪ ▪ ▪

400 g (14 oz) spaghetti or linguine
100 g (3½ oz) unsalted butter, softened
6 anchovy fillets, finely chopped or mashed
2 garlic cloves, minced
1 small red chilli, finely chopped (optional)
zest and juice of 1 lemon
2 tablespoons finely chopped parsley
grated parmesan, to serve (optional)

Bring a large pan of generously salted water to the boil. Add the pasta and cook until al dente, following the packet directions. Drain, keeping 125 ml (½ cup) of the pasta water, then return to the hot pan.

While the pasta cooks, make an anchovy butter. Mash the softened butter with the anchovies, garlic and chilli (if using) until smooth. Add to the cooked pasta, tossing until well coated. Stir in a little of the pasta water to make a silky sauce.

Stir in the lemon zest, juice and parsley. Serve immediately, with parmesan and pepper if you like.

Butter pilaf with almonds and sultanas

This pilaf is all about contrasts – buttery grains of rice, sweet pops of sultanas and the crunch of almonds. It's a side dish that often steals the show. You can swap the almonds for pistachios, and the sultanas for dried apricots or dates. The turmeric is optional – it's just here for its vibrant colour.

▪ ▪ ▪ SERVES 4–6 ▪ ▪ ▪

400 g (2 cups) basmati or long-grain rice
3 tablespoons unsalted butter
1 small onion, finely chopped
2 garlic cloves, minced
½ teaspoon ground cinnamon
½ teaspoon ground cumin
½ teaspoon ground turmeric (optional)
875 ml (3½ cups) hot chicken or vegetable stock
60 g (½ cup) sultanas
60 g (½ cup) slivered almonds, lightly toasted
chopped parsley or coriander (cilantro) leaves, to serve

Rinse the rice under cold water until the water runs clear. Soak in a bowl of water for 15 minutes, then drain well.

Melt the butter in a heavy-based saucepan over medium heat. Add the onion and cook for 5 minutes or until soft and translucent. Stir in the garlic, cinnamon, cumin and turmeric (if using), and cook until fragrant. Add the rice and stir to coat in the buttery spices.

Pour in the hot stock and bring to the boil. Stir in the sultanas, reduce to the lowest heat, cover tightly and cook for 15 minutes. Remove from the heat and leave covered for 10 minutes to finish steaming.

Fluff the rice gently with a fork, fold in the almonds and season with salt and pepper. Garnish with parsley to serve.

Freekeh with ghee and pomegranate

Freekeh's smoky flavour pairs beautifully with the richness of ghee and jewel-like, juicy pomegranate seeds. This is a dish that achieves a rare double – it's both fresh, yet hearty. Top with grilled chicken or lamb, or roasted vegetables, to turn it into a main dish.

▪ ▪ ▪ SERVES 4 ▪ ▪ ▪

2 tablespoons ghee
1 small onion, finely chopped
2 garlic cloves, minced
½ teaspoon ground cumin
½ teaspoon ground coriander
200 g (1 cup) cracked freekeh, rinsed
500 ml (2 cups) hot vegetable or chicken stock
60 g (½ cup) pomegranate seeds
60 g (¼ cup) toasted pine nuts or slivered almonds
2 tablespoons chopped mint leaves
2 tablespoons chopped parsley

Heat the ghee in a saucepan over medium heat. Add the onion and cook for 5 minutes or until soft and golden. Stir in the garlic, cumin and coriander and cook for 1 minute until fragrant.

Add the freekeh and stir well to coat in the ghee and spices. Pour in the hot stock, bring to the boil, then reduce the heat to low. Cover and simmer for 20 minutes, or until the freekeh is tender and has absorbed the liquid. Remove from heat and leave, covered, for 5 minutes.

Fluff the freekeh with a fork and fold in the pomegranate seeds, nuts, mint and parsley. Season with salt and pepper and serve warm or at room temperature.

CHICKEN, BEEF AND LAMB

Chicken and leek shortcrust pie from Madeleine Butter

Jack Gaffney, founder of Madeleine Butter, has earned a reputation for crafting beautifully cultured, small-batch butter that celebrates tradition and technique. With a background in fine food and a passion for honest, simple ingredients, Jack brings the same care to his kitchen as he does to his churn. Here he shares one of his family favourites, which is even better when prepared with Madeleine Butter, if it's available near you. 'We're big fans of pies in our home,' Jack says. 'Especially when we make the pastry ourselves.'

▪ ▪ ▪ SERVES 4–6 ▪ ▪ ▪

375 g (2½ cups) plain (all-purpose) flour, plus extra for dusting
1 teaspoon sea salt
340 g (12 oz) unsalted cultured butter, chilled and diced
60 ml (¼ cup) ice-cold water

FILLING
60 g (2 oz) unsalted cultured butter
2 tablespoons olive oil
550 g (1 lb 3 oz) chicken thighs, bone-in, skin-on
peel of 1 lemon
6 thyme sprigs
4 garlic cloves, minced
150 ml (5 fl oz) white wine, such as riesling
200 ml (7 fl oz) chicken stock
100 ml (3½ fl oz) double (heavy) cream
1 tablespoon Dijon mustard
2 leeks, white part only, finely chopped
1 egg, lightly beaten

To make the pastry, whisk the flour and salt in a large bowl. Add the butter and rub in with your fingertips until the mixture is like grains of sand. Work quickly to keep the butter cold. Drizzle in the ice-cold water and bring the dough together with your hands. Be careful not to overwork the dough – it's ready when you squeeze it together and it holds.

Divide the dough in two, one part slightly larger than the other. Flatten into discs, wrap each in plastic wrap and refrigerate for at least 1 hour.

Take the larger dough disc out of the fridge and set aside – it will soften up in about 15 minutes. Dust your work surface with flour and roll out the dough large enough to line a greased 23–25 cm (9–10 in) pie tin, then return to the fridge.

To make the filling, melt the butter with 1 tablespoon of the olive oil in a large frying pan over medium heat. Add the chicken thighs, lemon peel and thyme sprigs, season well and cook for about 5 minutes. Add the garlic and cook for 1 minute, then add the wine. Allow the alcohol to cook off for 2 minutes and then add the stock. Stir in the cream and mustard. Bring to a gentle simmer, season again if required, then cover and cook for 20 minutes.

Heat the remaining olive oil in a separate frying pan and cook the leek over low heat for about 20 minutes or until very soft, stirring occasionally.

Lift out the chicken from the first pan and set aside to cool. Discard the thyme springs and lemon peel but continue to simmer the sauce, uncovered, for 2–3 minutes, or until it has reduced and thickened a little. Remove from the heat.

Shred the chicken, discarding any bones and skin. Add the leek and shredded chicken to the thickened sauce and stir together.

Meanwhile, preheat the oven to 200°C (400°F) fan-forced.

Take the pastry base and dough disc out of the fridge. Line the pastry base with baking paper and fill with pie weights or uncooked rice or beans. Bake for 15 minutes or until the edges are set. Remove the paper and weights.

Brush the inside and edge of the pastry shell with some of the egg wash. Return to the oven for 5 minutes. Remove from the oven and increase the temperature to 220°C (430°F).

Spoon the filling into the pastry shell. Roll out the second dough disc and slice into strips. Lay the strips across the top of the pie in a lattice pattern. Brush the top generously with the remaining egg wash. Bake for 30 minutes or until the pastry is golden, and enjoy warm.

Buttermilk roast chicken

Buttermilk is to chicken what butter is to bread – a perfect partner. Marinating chicken in buttermilk tenderises it – an overnight soak works best, as the enzymes in the buttermilk break down the proteins in the meat, creating a velvety texture and delivering a satisfyingly juicy roast.

▪ ▪ ▪ SERVES 6 ▪ ▪ ▪

- 500 ml (2 cups) cultured buttermilk (see Tip on page 106)
- 2 garlic cloves, crushed
- 2 tablespoons chopped rosemary leaves
- 1 tablespoon sea salt flakes, plus extra to sprinkle
- 1 teaspoon smoked paprika, plus extra to sprinkle
- 1.5–2 kg (3–4 lb) chicken
- 2 tablespoons ghee or olive oil
- Perfectly crisp ghee-roasted potatoes (page 127), to serve (optional)

Stir together the buttermilk, garlic, rosemary, salt and paprika in a large glass bowl (avoid metal or plastic). Gently add the chicken, turning it over to coat well with the mixture. Cover the bowl with plastic wrap or a dinner plate and leave in the fridge to marinate overnight or for up to 24 hours.

Preheat the oven to 200°C (400°F) fan-forced.

Lift out the chicken from the marinade and pat dry with paper towel. Lay the chicken breast-side-up in a large roasting tin and drizzle the ghee over the chicken and tin. Sprinkle the chicken with the salt and, if desired, extra paprika.

Roast the chicken for 45 minutes to 1 hour, or until the skin is golden brown and the juices run clear when you prick the chicken thigh with a skewer. Leave to rest for 10 minutes before carving.

Serve with your choice of sides, such as ghee-roasted potatoes.

JONNY CRICKMORE

Bungay Butter, Fen Farm Dairy

SUFFOLK, ENGLAND

. . .

THE QUIET REVOLUTION ON FEN FARM

Bungay is the kind of butter that celebrity chefs such as Nigella Lawson and Jamie Oliver keep in their fridges. The milk comes warm, straight from the milking, drawn from the farm's grass-fed Montbéliarde cows. The Crickmore family are self-confessed stewards of this land in Suffolk and put the ecosystem, animal welfare and community at the heart of everything they do. They have even created a cowpat heat exchange system, biomass boiler and solar battery storage. This is butter with a zero-carbon footprint – you can't get any better than that.

Speaking to Jonny Crickmore, I find a grounded ease to him – the kind that comes from spending a lifetime on this land. Fen Farm has been in his family for three generations, but the dairy that Jonny runs today looks nothing like the one he inherited. Where many UK dairies have scaled, consolidated or disappeared, Jonny took a different route: smaller, better, braver.

Fen Farm's now-famous Bungay Butter didn't begin as a marketing idea. It began with Jonny's fascination with raw, grass-fed milk and the flavours it could hold when treated gently. He wanted to make butter the way traditional Suffolk farmers had done in the past – slow-churned, naturally cultured and with the milk's identity intact. Inspiration came from Normandy and its old-world butter traditions, but the heart of it remained local: Suffolk cows, Suffolk pastures, Suffolk weather.

Jonny talks about butter with a cheese-maker's sensitivity – acidity curves, seasonal fat changes, and how the churn 'tells you' when it's ready. Fen Farm's approach is intentionally simple: minimal intervention for maximum flavour. Their butter is made from raw milk, cultured gently and churned to a texture that feels like something lifted straight from a farmhouse table.

Despite its international acclaim, Fen Farm still feels like a family operation. Dulcie Crickmore, Jonny's wife, handles much of the storytelling, their children wander in and out of the dairy, while visitors arrive, expecting a quick look, and leave with a sense that they've stepped into a place where craft genuinely matters.

For Jonny, Bungay Butter isn't just a product – it's a way of keeping his land, his cows and his community at the centre of the story.

Bungay butter chicken from Fen Farm Dairy

This Bungay butter chicken comes straight from Fen Farm Dairy, shared lovingly by Jonny and his family, who learnt the recipe through their close friendship with a local Kenyan Sikh family. If you're not lucky enough to have a block of Jonny's butter on hand, any good unsalted artisan butter will still do the recipe proud.

▪ ▪ ▪ SERVES 6–8 ▪ ▪ ▪

20 g (¾ oz) ginger, peeled
2 green chillies
8 garlic cloves
2 tablespoons salt
2 teaspoons Kashmiri chilli powder
1 tablespoon cumin powder
2 teaspoons garam masala
1 tablespoon lemon juice
1 tablespoon vegetable oil
100 g (3½ oz) plain yoghurt
1 kg (2 lb 3 oz) boneless, skinless chicken thighs, cubed
40 g (1½ oz) unsalted cultured butter, melted
rice or Paratha (page 186), to serve

SAUCE
185 ml (¾ cup) vegetable oil
12 garlic cloves
2–3 long green chillies
50 g (1¾ oz) ginger, minced
3 bay leaves
10 green cardamon pods
3 black cardamon pods
1 tablespoon cumin seeds
1 tablespoon ground cumin
3 cinnamon sticks
2 teaspoons salt
2 tablespoons tomato paste (concentrated puree)
800 g (1 lb 12 oz) tinned chopped tomatoes
50 g (1¾ oz) unsalted cultured butter
4 teaspoons garam masala
30 g (1 oz) jaggery or brown sugar
1½ tablespoons honey
1 tablespoon dried fenugreek leaves
110 ml (4 fl oz) double (heavy) cream

Put the ginger, chillies and garlic in a food processor and blitz until finely mixed. Transfer to a large glass bowl, add the salt, chilli powder, cumin, garam masala, lemon juice, vegetable oil and yoghurt and stir together. Add the chicken, cover with plastic wrap or a dinner plate and marinate in the fridge for at least 2 hours but preferably 24 hours.

To make the sauce, heat the oil in a frying pan over medium heat and fry the garlic, chillies and ginger for 4–5 minutes until fragrant. Add the bay leaves, green and black cardamon pods, cumin seeds, ground cumin, cinnamon sticks and salt and sizzle in the oil for a few minutes until you can smell the aroma. Take care not to burn them.

Add the tomato paste and cook for 10 minutes or until the oil separates. Blitz the tomatoes until smooth and add to the pan. Bring to the boil, then reduce the heat and leave to simmer for 30 minutes.

Add the butter and simmer for another 5 minutes. Add the garam masala, jaggery, honey, dried fenugreek and simmer for another 5 minutes. Increase the heat to bring to the boil, then reduce the heat again, add the cream and simmer for 10 minutes.

Meanwhile, preheat the grill to high and place the chicken on a baking tray. Brush with the melted butter and place under the hot grill for 10 minutes until cooked through and charred. Add the cooked chicken to the sauce and stir through before serving over rice or with paratha.

Butter-tossed steak bites with rosemary and smoked salt

Fast, fun and wildly delicious, this is butter-forward cooking at its best. Bite-sized beef tossed in sizzling butter, rosemary and garlic, then finished with smoked salt – this makes a perfect snack with crusty bread, or a full meal piled onto buttery mash.

▪ ▪ ▪ SERVES 2–3 ▪ ▪ ▪

500 g (1 lb 2 oz) rump, sirloin or scotch fillet, cut into 2 cm (¾ in) cubes
2 tablespoons olive oil
85 g (3 oz) salted cultured butter
2 garlic cloves, minced
1 rosemary sprig
smoked salt, to serve

Season the beef with plenty of salt and pepper.

Heat the oil in a heavy-based frying pan over high heat. Fry the beef in batches, tossing, for 1–2 minutes until caramelised. Transfer to a plate as you caramelise the other batches so you don't overcrowd the pan.

Return all the beef to the pan and add the butter, garlic and rosemary. Toss to coat the beef for 30 seconds – keep the pan very hot (a fast cook results in tender steak). Serve immediately, sprinkled with smoked salt.

Lamb cutlets with anchovy-herb butter

Anchovies in butter is pure magic – salty and silky with a savoury richness. Paired with sweet lamb cutlets, it feels fancy without any fuss. This is a favourite in our house for Saturday lunch or as a quick weeknight indulgence.

▪ ▪ ▪ SERVES 4 ▪ ▪ ▪

12 lamb cutlets
1 tablespoon olive oil
85 g (3 oz) salted butter
lemon wedges, to serve (optional)

ANCHOVY-HERB BUTTER
100 g (3½ oz) unsalted cultured butter, softened
4 anchovy fillets, finely chopped
1 tablespoon capers, chopped
1 tablespoon chopped parsley leaves
zest of ½ lemon
pinch of chilli flakes (optional)

Mix together all the ingredients for the anchovy-herb butter. Set aside.

Season the lamb with salt and pepper. Heat the oil in a frying pan over medium-high heat. Add the lamb cutlets and sear for 2–3 minutes each side. Add the salted butter to the pan and continue cooking the lamb, basting with the butter, for 1–2 minutes.

Remove the pan from the heat, spoon the anchovy-herb butter over the lamb and let it melt for a minute or two before serving with lemon wedges, if desired.

BERTAIN
PINO
20
23
NOI

PIERRE 'PEPE' ISSA

Pepe Saya

SYDNEY, AUSTRALIA

. . .

THE RELUCTANT PIONEER OF CULTURED BUTTER

Pepe Saya has the kind of unpolished charm that instantly puts you at ease. This is a man who approaches both butter and people with the same gentle humility.

Pepe never set out to become Australia's butter mascot, but that's exactly what has happened. When he began making cultured butter in 2010, very few people knew what it was. But he had goals, and one of the first was simply: *'Guillaume Brahimi must call us.'* When that call eventually came from the award-winning chef at the Sydney Opera House's Bennelong restaurant, Pepe knew something had shifted. People were finally understanding cultured butter's complexity.

Despite his French name, Pepe is not French. His approach has been shaped by Australian dairy – informed by European tradition, rather than inherited from it. Before butter, Pepe ran a successful dairy dessert business – pannacotta, tiramisu, mousses and baked desserts. He had no formal training in butter-making, and the business itself was born almost accidentally. In 2009, faced with excess cream before a holiday shutdown, he churned butter to avoid waste. The result wasn't amazing, but it sparked a question: why did imported French butter taste so much better?

That question became the foundation of Pepe Saya Butter. Through research, conversations and guidance from dairy specialists, Pepe began experimenting with culturing cream before churning – a process largely absent from Australian butter at the time.

From the outset, the business focused on cultured butter, shaped by hand into its now-distinctive round form – a practical decision born from hand-packing rather than branding. Pepe first sold his butter at farmers' markets and to retailers, building awareness through chefs rather than supermarkets. Although Brahimi's call validated Pepe's work, Pepe was reluctant to pursue a deeper collaboration, wary of aligning his brand with French culinary authority rather than championing Australian butter on its own terms. That decision reflects a core principle of his business: to prove that Australian cream, handled with care, can stand confidently alongside the best.

Exporting butter is another story: 'madness,' he laughs. Dairy exporters pay eye-watering fees long before a single gram of butter even leaves the country. That's why he now divides his time between Australia and the US, while Melissa, his wife and CEO, 'runs Sydney.' Together, they're building a small Australian butter company with global reach.

What stands out most about Pepe is his unwavering passion. Sixteen years in, he talks about cream quality like someone who fell in love yesterday. He's a teacher at heart – one brick in the long road to helping Australia rediscover how good butter can be.

He encourages me in my own butter journey. 'Get out there as much as you can,' he says. 'That's the way to do it.' It feels like advice, but also a kind of blessing, from one butter devotee to another.

Cottage pie from Pepe Saya

This recipe comes from fellow butter-maker Pepe Saya, whose commitment to Australian dairy and beautiful cultured butter has inspired so many cooks and producers across the country. The pie is a true reflection of Pepe's style – simple, comforting and the kind of dish that brings people to the table. If you can, try to make it with his butter and crème fraîche.

▪ ▪ ▪ SERVES 6 ▪ ▪ ▪

250 g (9 oz) plain (all-purpose) flour, plus extra for dusting
pinch of salt
125 g (4 oz) unsalted cultured butter, chilled and diced
1–3 tablespoons ice-cold water

FILLING
1 tablespoon olive oil
1 onion, finely diced
1 carrot, grated or diced
2 garlic cloves, minced
1 celery stalk, diced
310 ml (1¼ cups) chicken gravy
2 tablespoons Worcestershire sauce
2 tablespoons HP sauce or smoky BBQ sauce
500 g (1 lb 2 oz) minced (ground) beef or lamb

TOPPING
4–5 Pontiac potatoes, peeled and chopped
4 tablespoons crème fraîche
60 g (2 oz) salted cultured butter
2 teaspoons smoked paprika
1 tablespoon breadcrumbs

To make the pastry, sift the flour and salt into a large bowl or food processor. Add the butter and rub into the flour with your fingertips, or pulse in the food processor, until the mixture resembles breadcrumbs.

Slowly add the chilled water, a tablespoon at a time, until the mixture comes together to form a dough. Tip out onto a lightly floured surface and bring together into a ball with your hands. Wrap in plastic wrap and chill for at least 30 minutes.

Grease and line an 18 × 28 cm (7 × 11 in) baking dish with baking paper and roll out the pastry large enough to line it. Prick the base of the pastry with a fork, then cover with plastic wrap and refrigerate for 20 minutes.

Meanwhile, to make the filling, heat the oil in a large frying pan or flameproof casserole dish (Dutch oven) over low heat. Add the onion, carrot, garlic and celery and cook gently for about 5 minutes or until softened. Stir in the gravy, Worcestershire sauce, HP sauce and mince, and cook for around 30 minutes, breaking up any lumps with a wooden spoon, until the meat has browned and any excess liquid has evaporated.

To make the topping, cook the potato in a large saucepan of boiling water for 10–15 minutes or until tender. Drain, return to the pan and mash the potato until smooth. Add the crème fraîche and butter and season well with salt and pepper.

Preheat the oven to 200°C (400°F) fan-forced.

Remove the pastry base from the fridge and line with baking paper. Fill with pie weights or uncooked rice or beans and blind bake for 15 minutes. Remove the paper and pie weights and carefully spoon the filling into the pastry base.

Top with dollops of creamy mashed potato and sprinkle with smoked paprika and breadcrumbs. Bake for 15 minutes to brown the top of the pie and serve immediately.

SEAFOOD

Smoked salmon with potato scones and cultured butter hollandaise from The Edinburgh Butter Co.

Here is a lovely Scottish-influenced recipe from Chloe and her team at The Edinburgh Butter Co. In Scotland, potato scones – affectionately known as 'tattie scones' – are a staple of the traditional bacon-and-egg fried breakfast, but they're also often paired with smoked salmon or trout. Served with hollandaise, this is a perfect weekend brunch, with the cultured butter adding a rich, tangy depth to the sauce.

▪ ▪ ▪ SERVES 4 ▪ ▪ ▪

200 g (7 oz) smoked salmon or trout
1 tablespoon chopped dill
½ lemon, cut into wedges

POTATO SCONES
500 g (1 lb 2 oz) floury potatoes, peeled and quartered
50 g (1¾ oz) butter, plus extra for frying
150 g (5½ oz) plain (all-purpose) flour, plus extra for dusting
1 teaspoon baking powder
1 egg, lightly beaten

HOLLANDAISE SAUCE
100 g (3½ oz) salted cultured butter
2 egg yolks
1 tablespoon white wine vinegar
juice of ½ lemon

To make the scones, place the potato in a saucepan and cover generously with cold water. Bring to the boil and cook for about 20 minutes, until tender. Drain and return to the hot pan to dry the potato out slightly. Transfer to a bowl and mash with a potato ricer or masher, then return to the pan. Add the butter and season with salt and pepper.

Put the mash, flour and baking powder in a bowl and mix well with a wooden spoon. Add the egg and combine to make a soft dough. Depending on how moist your mash is, you may need more or less flour. If it seems a little sticky, add some more flour until the dough comes away from the side of the bowl.

Turn out onto a well-floured surface and knead softly to bring the dough together. Divide into 3 balls. Roll each dough ball into a circle about 20 cm (8 in) in diameter and 5 mm (¼ in) thick. Then cut each circle into 4 equal triangles.

Warm a non-stick frying pan over medium heat. Once hot, add a little butter and 4 triangles to the pan. Cook for about 4–5 minutes on each side – once the underside of the scones are golden brown, flip and cook the other side. Remove from the pan and allow to cool while you cook the rest.

To make the hollandaise, melt the butter in a small saucepan over low heat. Once the butter is foaming, remove the pan from the heat and leave to cool slightly – the milk solids will sink to the bottom of the pan.

Put the egg yolks and vinegar in a heatproof bowl set over a pan of simmering water (do not allow the base of the bowl to touch the water) and whisk with a balloon whisk. The heat needs to be low so the eggs don't scramble.

Whisk until the eggs are lukewarm, then add the melted butter slowly, whisking constantly, until only the white solids are left at the bottom of the pan. You should now have a smooth, velvety sauce. Season with lemon juice, salt and white pepper.

Serve the scones topped with smoked salmon and hollandaise, scattered with the dill and with the lemon wedges on the side.

Hollandaise is best served fresh although it can be stored in an airtight container in the fridge for up to 24 hours. Never freeze it. Store the scones in an airtight container at room temperature for up to 2 days. Reheat in the oven (not the microwave) at 160°C (320°F) for 5–8 minutes.

Buttermilk tartar sauce for a seafood platter

I love buttermilk for its versatility, especially the bright acidity you get from fresh cultured buttermilk. The supermarket versions don't carry that same tang, so the flavour never quite compares.

▪ ▪ ▪ SERVES 6 ▪ ▪ ▪

cold seafood platter or prawns (shrimp), to serve

BUTTERMILK TARTAR SAUCE
80 ml (⅓ cup) mayonnaise
2 tablespoons cultured buttermilk (see Tip on page 106)
2 teaspoons lemon juice
1 teaspoon Dijon mustard
3 tablespoons dill pickles (gherkins), finely chopped
2 tablespoons capers, chopped
1 garlic clove, minced

Mix all the sauce ingredients together until well combined. Cover and refrigerate for 30 minutes. Serve with seafood.

Store the tartar sauce in an airtight container in the fridge for 3–4 days. Keep it chilled during serving and avoid freezing, as the buttermilk and mayonnaise will separate.

Lobster with herb butter

The rich creaminess of this melted butter enhances the sweet, delicate texture of the lobster. A perfect dish for sharing at a hot Australian Christmas dinner, it's great with a leafy salad and crusty bread. With fresh lobster as the hero ingredient, it only requires a few quick and simple steps – my kind of recipe! If you'd like a deeper, nuttier flavour, warm the butter in a pan until it just begins to brown before adding the herbs – the nuttiness of brown butter works beautifully with lobster.

▪ ▪ ▪ SERVES 4 ▪ ▪ ▪

25 g (½ cup) chopped parsley
15 g (¼ cup) chopped dill
2 garlic cloves, minced
150 g (5½ oz) salted butter, at room temperature
4 cooked lobsters, halved lengthways
lemon wedges, to serve

Preheat the grill to medium–hot.

Mix together the herbs and garlic and then mix thoroughly into the softened butter. Season with salt and pepper.

Place the lobster halves on a baking tray. Spread each half with garlic–herb butter, then place under the hot grill for 4–5 minutes, basting with more butter as they warm through. The lobster is already cooked so you're just heating it and letting the butter flavour the meat.

Transfer to a platter, pour over more herb butter and finish with a squeeze of lemon. Serve immediately with lemon wedges on the side.

Garlic prawns with fresh herbs

To me, garlic prawns are a quintessential summer dish: quick to cook, rich in flavour and best eaten straight from the pool of golden butter in the pan. Just add the best bread and butter you can find and dinner is sorted. Alternatively, toss through cooked linguine to turn it into a bigger meal.

▪ ▪ ▪ SERVES 4 ▪ ▪ ▪

1 kg (2 lb 3 oz) raw prawns (shrimp), peeled and deveined
1 tablespoon olive oil
100 g (3½ oz) salted cultured butter
4 garlic cloves, minced
60 ml (¼ cup) dry white wine or chicken stock
zest and juice of 1 lemon
2 tablespoons chopped parsley
1 tablespoon chopped chives
lemon wedges, to serve

Pat the prawns dry with paper towel and season lightly with salt.

Heat a large frying pan over medium–high heat and add the olive oil and half the butter. Once the butter melts and foams, add the prawns to the pan and cook for 1–2 minutes on each side, until pink and just cooked through.

Reduce the heat slightly and add the garlic. Cook gently for 30 seconds until fragrant but not browned. Add the white wine, lemon zest and juice, and the remaining butter. Swirl the pan until the butter melts into a glossy sauce.

Sprinkle with the parsley and chives, season with plenty of pepper and serve with lemon wedges and bread for mopping up the buttery sauce.

Brown butter snapper with capers and sage

Fresh fish and butter feel like home here where I live on the coast. This is one of my favourite recipes – simple, quick and perfectly balanced. The toasty brown butter brings warmth and depth, while the lemon and capers cut through the richness with a bright, tart burst. I recommend enjoying with buttery mashed potatoes, as they soak up the sauce perfectly.

▪ ▪ ▪ SERVES 2–4 ▪ ▪ ▪

- 4 snapper fillets or other firm white fish
- 3 tablespoons plain (all-purpose) flour, for dusting
- 1 tablespoon olive oil
- 100 g (3½ oz) unsalted butter
- 2 tablespoons baby capers
- 6–8 sage leaves
- juice of ½ lemon
- Mashed potatoes Robuchon-style, to serve (page 130; optional)

Pat the fish dry and season both sides with salt and pepper. Dust lightly with the flour, shaking off the excess.

Heat the olive oil and half the butter in a large non-stick pan over medium heat. When the butter foams, add the fish, skin side down. Cook for 3–4 minutes per side until golden and cooked through. Transfer to a warm plate.

Wipe the pan clean, add the remaining butter and cook over medium heat, swirling the pan often, until the butter foams and turns a golden brown with a nutty aroma – watch it closely. Toss in the capers and sage leaves, letting them sizzle for 30 seconds. Remove from the heat immediately and stir in the lemon juice.

Spoon the brown butter, capers and sage over the fish and serve immediately with your sides of choice, such as mashed potatoes.

Scallops with cultured butter, seaweed and white wine sauce

Scallops have always been my husband's favourite. Whenever they're on a menu, I know what Mike's ordering. We are lucky enough to be able to buy scallops from a boat moored at the pier in a nearby coastal town, Queenscliff.

This is Mike's favourite way to cook them – sweet golden scallops finished in a silky sauce of cultured butter and chardonnay. Simple to make, they're an indulgent treat for our butter factory's number one fan. For a dramatic finish, serve on warmed scallop shells.

▪ ▪ ▪ SERVES 4 ▪ ▪ ▪

- 2 tablespoons olive oil
- 12 large scallops
- 1 small French shallot, finely diced
- 60 ml (¼ cup) chardonnay or another dry white wine
- 100 g (3½ oz) salted cultured butter, diced
- 1 teaspoon finely shredded nori or dried seaweed flakes
- 1 tablespoon lemon juice
- chopped chives or micro herbs, to garnish

Heat the olive oil in a large non-stick frying pan over high heat. Pat the scallops dry with paper towel, season lightly with salt and pepper and then add to the pan in a single layer. Cook for 1–1½ minutes on each side until golden. Remove all the scallops to a plate and keep warm.

Reduce the heat to medium. Add the shallot to the pan and cook gently for about 1 minute until softened. Pour in the wine and let it bubble for 30 seconds, scraping up any browned bits.

Whisk in the butter, a few cubes at a time, until it melts into a silky sauce. Add the seaweed and lemon juice and season to taste. Spoon the sauce over the scallops and garnish with chives to serve.

BAKING AND SWEET THINGS

Buttermilk pancakes with caramel sauce

Who doesn't love pancakes? The best recipes must include buttermilk to ensure a fluffy crumb. The fluffier the better to soak up this caramel sauce, I say! Buttermilk also gives the sauce a subtle tang and gorgeous depth – not too sweet, perfectly silky, totally addictive. It's also great on apple cake, or bread and butter pudding, with poached peaches, as a dip for fresh strawberries... and occasionally straight off the spoon when no one's looking! If you don't have time to make the sauce, a dollop of cultured butter and maple syrup is always an acceptable substitute.

▪ ▪ ▪ SERVES 4 ▪ ▪ ▪

300 g (2 cups) plain (all-purpose) flour
3 tablespoons caster (superfine) sugar
1½ teaspoons baking powder
1 teaspoon baking soda
1 teaspoon salt
625 ml (2½ cups) cultured buttermilk (see Tip on page 106)
2 large eggs
3 tablespoons unsalted butter, melted, plus extra for greasing and to serve (optional)
mascarpone, to serve (optional)

BUTTERMILK CARAMEL SAUCE
200 g (1 cup) caster (superfine) sugar
125 ml (½ cup) cultured buttermilk
60 g (2 oz) unsalted cultured butter
¼ teaspoon baking soda
1 teaspoon vanilla extract
pinch of sea salt

To make the buttermilk caramel sauce, whisk together the sugar and buttermilk in a saucepan. Add the butter and gently bring to the boil over medium heat. Once bubbling, whisk in the baking soda – the mixture will foam up (this creates lightness and keeps it smooth). Cook for 6–8 minutes, stirring occasionally, until deep golden and slightly thickened. The sauce will thicken further as it cools. Remove from heat and stir in the vanilla and salt. Allow to cool slightly before serving.

To make the pancakes, whisk together the flour, sugar, baking powder, baking soda and salt in a large bowl. Make a well in the centre and pour in the buttermilk. Crack the eggs into the buttermilk and add the melted butter.

Starting from the centre, whisk gently to draw in the dry ingredients from the sides until just combined. Don't overmix – a few small lumps are perfectly fine. You can cover and refrigerate the batter for up to an hour now if you want to make it in advance.

Warm a non-stick or cast-iron frying pan over low heat for about 5 minutes to warm through. Add a little oil or butter to coat the surface, then increase the heat to medium–low. Pour about 80 ml (⅓ cup) of batter per pancake into the pan, cooking one or two at a time depending on your pan size.

After 2–4 minutes, when small bubbles appear on the surface and the edges begin to brown, flip the pancakes and cook until golden on the other side. Remove from the pan and keep warm while you cook the rest.

Serve the pancakes with the caramel sauce. For a bit of extra indulgence, finish with butter or a dollop of mascarpone.

Store the sauce in a sealed jar in the fridge for up to 2 weeks. Warm gently before serving.

Variation

Swap 150 g (1 cup) of the flour for 100 g (1 cup) lightly blitzed rolled oats to make heartier, nutty oatcakes that are great with cultured butter, honey and berries. Let the batter rest for 10 minutes before cooking.

Banana bread

My youngest son, Archie, loves bananas but, like most families, we do end up with a few overripe ones sitting forlornly on the kitchen bench. This is my go-to, no-fail recipe for using them up. If you change the flour to something 'healthier', such as a spelt or rye flour, it yields a beautiful dense bread. I love the inclusion of fermented dairy such as buttermilk or crème fraîche here. Credit for this recipe goes to Sally's Baking Addiction, with some small changes from me. Try this with a flavoured butter, perhaps chocolate espresso or salted caramel **on pages 87 and 88.**

▪ ▪ ▪ SERVES 8–12 ▪ ▪ ▪

300 g (2 cups) plain (all-purpose) flour
1 teaspoon baking soda
¼ teaspoon salt
½ teaspoon ground cinnamon
115 g (½ cup) unsalted cultured butter, softened, plus extra to serve (optional)
150 g (¾ cup) light or dark brown sugar
2 large eggs
80 ml (⅓ cup) buttermilk, at room temperature
3–4 ripe bananas (1½ cups mashed)
1 teaspoon vanilla extract
90 g (¾ cup) chopped walnuts, 90 g (¾ cup) sultanas (golden raisins) or 180 g (1 cup) chocolate buttons (optional)

Place a rack low down in the oven and preheat the oven to 180°C (350°F) fan-forced. Grease a 24 × 12 cm (9 × 5 in) loaf tin.

Whisk together the flour, baking soda, salt and cinnamon and set aside.

Beat the butter and brown sugar together with electric beaters or hand beaters for about 3 minutes until light and creamy. Add the eggs one at a time, beating well after each addition. Scrape down the side of the bowl as needed. Beat in the buttermilk, mashed bananas and vanilla.

Add the dry ingredients and beat on low speed just until combined – do not overmix. Fold in the walnuts, if using. The batter should be thick.

Spoon into the loaf tin and bake for 1 hour, covering loosely with foil after 30 minutes to prevent the top getting too brown. A skewer poked into the centre should come out clean with only a few small moist crumbs. Cool in the tin on a rack for 1 hour, then remove from the tin and cool completely before slicing to serve. Enjoy with butter, if desired.

Store the banana bread in an airtight container at room temperature for up to 3 days. For longer storage, slice the loaf, wrap the pieces individually in baking paper, and freeze in an airtight container for up to 3 months. Thaw at room temperature or warm slices in the oven or toaster straight from frozen.

Buttermilk buns

The first time I saw these buns being made by one of the bakers we supply with fresh buttermilk, I was captivated. Their golden-brown glossy tops are striking, and the delicacy of their light, tender crumb is unforgettable. They remind me of brioche, but with an even softer, airier texture.

Ideally, you want cultured buttermilk here, but if you can't find one, just check the Tip on page 106.

▪ ▪ ▪ MAKES 20 ▪ ▪ ▪

- 250 ml (1 cup) buttermilk, at room temperature
- 2–3 tablespoons milk
- 3 tablespoons caster (superfine) sugar
- 7 g (¼ oz) dried yeast (or 20 g/ ¾ oz fresh)
- 60 g (2 oz) unsalted butter, softened, plus extra to serve (optional)
- 1 large egg
- 500 g (1 lb 2 oz) plain (all-purpose) flour
- 1 teaspoon fine sea salt
- 1 egg beaten with 1 tablespoon milk, for brushing

Mix together the buttermilk, milk, sugar and yeast in a large bowl. Whisk gently to dissolve the sugar and yeast, then set aside in a warm place for 5 minutes or until lightly foamy.

Add the butter, egg, flour and salt and mix until a soft dough forms. Turn out onto a lightly floured surface and knead for 8–10 minutes until smooth and elastic. Alternatively, knead in a stand mixer fitted with a dough hook for 5–6 minutes. The dough should be soft and slightly sticky.

Place the dough in a lightly greased bowl, cover with a clean tea towel and leave in a warm place for 1–1½ hours, or until doubled in size.

Gently knock back the dough (give it a punch to knock the air out of it), then divide into around 20 equal portions. Shape each piece into a smooth ball. Arrange the balls on a baking tray lined with baking paper, spacing them about 5 cm (2 in) apart. Cover again and leave for another 15–30 minutes until puffy.

Preheat the oven to 180°C (fan-forced).

Brush the bun tops with the egg wash and bake for 12–15 minutes until lightly golden. Cool on the tray for 5 minutes, then transfer to a wire rack. Enjoy warm with butter, if desired.

Store the buns in an airtight container at room temperature for up to 2 days. For longer storage, place baked buns in a paper or freezer bag and freeze for up to 2 months; thaw at room temperature and warm briefly in a low oven before serving.

Variations

Sweet buns: Stir 2 tablespoons white sugar and a handful of sultanas (golden raisins), currants or chopped dried fruit into the dough. Brush with melted butter and sprinkle with cinnamon sugar before baking.

Seeded buns: Roll the shaped buns in sesame, poppy or sunflower seeds before baking; brush with egg wash first to help them stick.

Cheese and herb buns: Fold 125 g (1 cup) grated cheddar and 2 tablespoons chopped herbs (parsley, chives or dill) through the dough.

Paratha

A staple in South Asian meals, parathas are a buttery, flaky, chewy flatbread. They're wonderful to have on hand in your freezer for pairing with a curry, soup or casseroles, but they are also delicious simply enjoyed as a snack.

▪ ▪ ▪ MAKES 8 ▪ ▪ ▪

450 g (3 cups) plain (all-purpose) flour, plus extra for dusting
2 teaspoons salt
2 tablespoons vegetable or canola oil
250 ml (1 cup) warm water
185 ml (¾ cup) ghee, at room temperature

Whisk together the flour and salt in a large bowl. Drizzle with 1 tablespoon of the oil and use your fingertips to rub the oil into the flour until the mixture looks like grains of sand.

Make a well in the centre and pour in the warm water. Mix with your hands until it begins to form one mass. Knead the dough in the bowl until all the flour is incorporated – it will look lumpy but do not overwork it.

Leaving the dough in the bowl, rub a light coating of oil over its surface. Press a sheet of plastic wrap directly onto the surface and leave to rest for about 30 minutes until the dough is hydrated, supple and holds the shape of an indentation when poked.

Turn the dough out onto a lightly floured work surface and divide into 8 pieces. Roll out one portion at a time with a rolling pin, keeping the remaining portions covered with plastic wrap. Roll each one into a very thin round about 35 cm (14 in) across (it doesn't need to be perfectly round). The dough should be so thin that you can faintly see the work surface through it.

Use your fingers to spread 1 tablespoon of the ghee evenly over the dough circle. Sprinkle a pinch or two of flour over the ghee. Roll up the dough tightly into a log and then coil the log into a round spiral. Cover with plastic wrap while you roll the remaining portions of dough. Leave them to rest for 15 minutes.

Working with one piece at a time and keeping the rest covered with plastic wrap, roll out each portion to about 15 cm (6 in) across. Transfer to a plate as you roll out the rest. If stacking the rolled portions, place baking paper between them to prevent sticking.

Heat a non-stick frying pan over medium heat. Add a portion of dough and cook for 2–3 minutes until it's beginning to turn opaque but not browning. Flip over and cook for 2–3 minutes until totally opaque but not brown. Flip again and cook for 1 minute more until opaque.

Add 1½ teaspoons of ghee to the pan. Move the paratha around, flipping as needed, until coated in ghee and then cook for 2 minutes each side until golden brown. Transfer to a plate and cook the rest, adding more ghee if needed and reducing the heat if the paratha is browning before the centre is cooked.

The dough can be made in advance and stored in an airtight container in the fridge for up to 2 days. Let it come to room temperature before rolling.

Store the paratha in an airtight container in a pantry for up to 3 days. Paratha can be frozen for 2 months, stacked in an airtight container with baking paper between them to prevent sticking.

Cheese and ham scones

This is a family favourite – we can never make enough! The scones are perfect for lunchboxes, after school or weekend brunches. Eat them just out of the oven, halved and spread with butter, or reheat by zapping them in the microwave for a few seconds. You can use chopped cooked bacon instead of the ham.

▪ ▪ ▪ MAKES 12–20, DEPENDING ON SIZE ▪ ▪ ▪

500 g (4 cups) self-raising flour
¼ teaspoon salt
80 g (3 oz) unsalted cultured butter, chilled and grated, plus extra to serve (optional)
185 g (1½ cups) grated cheddar cheese
150 g (1 cup) finely chopped ham
375 ml (1½ cups) cultured buttermilk, plus extra as needed (see Tip on page 106)

Preheat the oven to 220°C (430°F) fan-forced. Line a large baking tray with baking paper.

Sift the flour and salt into a large mixing bowl. Add the grated butter and cut in with a knife until the mixture has the consistency of breadcrumbs. Stir in the cheese and ham and make a well in the centre. Add the buttermilk and stir until the mixture comes together to form a dough. If still crumbly, add 1–2 teaspoons of extra buttermilk.

Knead the dough just enough to bring it together and spread on the baking tray. Cut the dough into equal pieces and space out a little on the tray.

Bake for 10 minutes until golden and leave to cool for a few minutes on a rack before tucking in! Enjoy with butter, if desired.

Store the scones in an airtight container in the fridge for up to 2 days. Zap in the microwave for 15 seconds to reheat. For longer storage, freeze, wrapped individually or in an airtight container, for up to 3 months. Reheat from frozen in a 160°C (320°F) oven until warmed through.

Mae McLean's buttery jam drops

This recipe comes from my sister-in-law, Janet. Once a city girl, she bravely swapped to a life on the land when she married my brother Julian, a dairy farmer. I've always admired how wholeheartedly she embraced country life, trading her teaching career for early mornings, gumboots and milking cows. This recipe was passed down by Janet's grandmother Mae, also a dairy farmer.

▪ ▪ ▪ MAKES 18 ▪ ▪ ▪

125 g (4½ oz) salted butter, at room temperature
125 g (4½ oz) caster (superfine) sugar
1 teaspoon vanilla extract
1 egg, lightly beaten
225 g (1½ cups) self-raising flour, sifted
shredded coconut, for coating
2 tablespoons plum or raspberry jam

Cream together the butter, sugar and vanilla with electric beaters or a wooden spoon until pale. Add the egg and beat well. Add the flour and mix until a dough forms (if your mixture is very soft, leave it in the fridge for 30 minutes to firm up).

Preheat the oven to 160°C (320°F) fan-forced and line two baking trays with baking paper.

Shape the dough into balls (around 4 teaspoonsful for each ball) and then roll in coconut. Arrange the coated balls on the trays, leaving room for the biscuits to spread. Use your fingertip to make a well in the centre of each and spoon about ¼ teaspoon of the jam into the hole. Try not to overfill them.

Bake for 10–12 minutes or until pale golden. Allow to cool a little on the trays and then cool completely on a wire rack.

Store the jam drops in an airtight container at room temperature for up to 1 week. Keep them in a cool, dry place so the jam stays set. For longer storage, freeze in an airtight container for up to 3 months; thaw at room temperature before serving.

The dough can also be made 2 days in advance of baking and kept in the fridge.

Brown butter chocolate chip cookies

I'm often drawn into a cookie debate with my son Theo – should they be crunchy or chewy? I'm Team Crunchy. Theo is Team Chewy. And neither of us is willing to budge. Happily, these brown butter cookies sit somewhere in between: crisp at the edges, but soft and gooey in the middle. In the end, we are both satisfied.

▪ ▪ ▪ MAKES 12 ▪ ▪ ▪

110 g (4 oz) unsalted butter
100 g (½ cup) light or dark brown sugar
60 g (2 oz) white sugar
1 large egg
½ teaspoon vanilla extract
150 g (1 cup) plain (all-purpose) flour
¼ teaspoon baking powder
¼ teaspoon baking soda
1 teaspoon salt
220 g (8 oz) dark or milk chocolate buttons

Line two baking trays with baking paper.

Melt the butter in a saucepan over medium heat and cook for 3–4 minutes, swirling and whisking often, until it foams, turns golden brown and smells nutty.

Pour the brown butter into a bowl and leave to cool for 20 minutes – too hot, and it will scramble your eggs.

Add the brown and white sugars to the cooled butter and mix well. Add the egg and whisk for 1–2 minutes until the mixture is pale and thickened (an electric mixer makes this quick work). Stir in the vanilla.

Sift in the flour, baking powder, baking soda and salt. Fold gently with a spatula, stopping when you can still see a few streaks of flour. Fold in the chocolate buttons.

Preheat the oven to 180°C (350°F) fan-forced.

Spoon the dough out onto the baking tray – around 6 cookies per tray. Bake for 11–13 minutes, until the edges are set (a little longer for crispier cookies). Remove and give the tray a firm tap on the bench to help the cookies settle.

Cool on the tray for 10 minutes, then transfer to a wire rack to cool completely.

Store the cookies in an airtight container at room temperature for up to 3 days.

Peanut butter crinkles

This recipe is from Mary, wife of Steve, our behind-the-scenes legend who keeps the butter factory ticking over. Steve's the one we call when something needs fixing, lifting, welding or coaxing back to life. And, while Steve keeps the factory running, it's Mary who keeps everyone sweet. Her biscuits are legendary – loved by Steve, adored by their grandkids, and never known to last more than a day.

▪ ▪ ▪ MAKES 20 ▪ ▪ ▪

125 g (4½ oz) salted butter
½ teaspoon vanilla extract
½ teaspoon lemon zest
80 g (⅓ cup) caster (superfine) sugar
80 g (⅓ cup) brown sugar
90 g (⅓ cup) crunchy peanut butter
185 g (1¼ cups) plain (all-purpose) flour
¾ teaspoon baking soda

Preheat the oven to 180°C (350°F) fan-forced and line baking tray with baking paper.

Cream together the butter, vanilla, lemon zest, sugars and peanut butter with electric beaters or a wooden spoon until pale. Add the sifted flour and baking soda and stir into a stiff dough.

Roll teaspoonfuls of dough into balls and place on the baking tray. Press down lightly with a fork, first across and then downwards, for a crinkled effect. Bake for 15 minutes until golden. Cool on a rack before eating.

Store the crinkles in an airtight container at room temperature for up to 5 days. For longer storage, freeze in an airtight container or freezer bag for up to 3 months. Thaw at room temperature or enjoy slightly warm after a few minutes in a low oven.

CHLOE BLACK

Director, The Edinburgh Butter Co.

EDINBURGH, SCOTLAND

. . .

CULTURED IN EDINBURGH

Founded in 2018 by Hilary and Nick Sinclair, The Edinburgh Butter Co. came out of a supper club and a shared passion for butter that transcends the ordinary. Talking to Chloe Black, Hilary's sister, you get the sense that the company grew in the same way as good cultured butter does – slowly, deliberately and with just the right amount of wildness.

It began not in a creamery, but in the tiny Edinburgh flat where Hilary and husband Nick ran the supper club. A trip to Sydney introduced them to cultured butter – and, unknowingly, planted the seed of a future business. Back home, they served their own homemade butter to guests, who immediately began asking if they could buy it. Soon delis were placing orders. Then the Balmoral Hotel called. Overnight, the kitchen hobby became a commitment.

They moved production to a makeshift urban creamery and later into a modest factory, where their equipment was given names and personalities of their own. The stainless-steel churn became Tina Churner – powerful, reliable and a little bit of a diva. The shaping machine was dubbed Shaun the Shaper, a quiet workhorse turning butter into perfect logs and sheets fit for Edinburgh's bakers and pastry chefs.

Chloe speaks of butter-making as equal parts precision and intuition. Their cream comes from England now, sourced from independent dairies, but its identity is defined in Edinburgh: in the culturing, the balancing of sweet and soured cream, the seasonal adjustments. Imperfections aren't flaws, she says – they're signs of real craft. They use traditional French methods: the cream is cultured into a thick, silky crème fraîche, then slow-churned in small batches to produce butter that is rich in flavour and texture.

Hats off to this talented crew, who don't just make butter, but also celebrate it.

They run Scotland's Best Croissant competition, where bakers from across the country rise to the challenge. Every entrant must use butter from The Edinburgh Butter Co. in a true showcase of its character. And, when Chloe sees a croissant lift in perfect layers, and knows that Tina Churner and Shaun the Shaper helped make it happen, that's when the whole journey makes sense.

The Edinburgh Butter
HOMEMADE FLAVOURED BUTTERS

Scottish shortbread from The Edinburgh Butter Co.

Let's be honest, a shortbread recipe should only be trusted if it comes from a Scot! Even better, from a Scottish butter-maker. To keep that signature crumbly texture, handle the dough as little as possible. Cut these into any shape you like, although fingers are our favourites – perfect for dunking into a hot cup of tea.

▪ ▪ ▪ MAKES 16 ▪ ▪ ▪

180 g (6½ oz) plain (all-purpose) flour, plus extra for dusting
50 g (¼ cup) caster (superfine) sugar, plus extra for dusting
125 g (4½ oz) unsalted cultured butter, chilled and diced

Line a large baking tray with baking paper.

Mix the flour and sugar together in a large bowl. Add the butter and rub in with your fingertips until the mixture looks like breadcrumbs. Bring the dough together into a ball and then roll out to about 1 cm (½ in) thick on a lightly floured surface.

Cut into whatever shapes you like and arrange on the baking tray. Prick the tops with a fork or flute the edges. Sprinkle with a little caster sugar and chill in the fridge for 20 minutes.

Meanwhile, preheat the oven to 160°C (320°F) fan-forced.

Bake the shortbread for 20–30 minutes until golden brown. Leave to cool a little on the tray before eating.

Store the shortbread in an airtight container at room temperature for up to 2 weeks. It keeps best in a cool, dry place. For longer storage, freeze in an airtight container for up to 3 months and thaw at room temperature before serving.

Honey crunches

If there's one recipe that sums up my childhood, this is it. Honey crunches – or honey joys, depending on who you ask – were a staple at every birthday party, school fete and cake stall. You had to be quick to grab one – and 20 cents was all it took! With just four ingredients, these are pure joy in a paper case. Even now, if I take a batch to a dinner party or morning tea, they disappear in seconds.

▪ ▪ ▪ MAKES 24 ▪ ▪ ▪

75 g (2¾ oz) salted butter
115 g (⅓ cup) honey
1 tablespoon caster (superfine) sugar
150 g (5 cups) cornflakes

Preheat the oven to 160°C (320°F) fan-forced. Line two 12-hole (⅓ cup) muffin trays with cupcake cases.

Stir the butter, honey and sugar in a small saucepan over low heat until smooth.

Tip the cornflakes into a large bowl, add the honey mixture and stir well. Spoon the mixture into the paper cases. Bake for 10 minutes and then leave to cool for 15 minutes to firm up before serving.

Store the honey crunches in an airtight container at room temperature for up to 24 hours.

Gabriel's almond and blueberry galette

As Gabriel Gaté says, 'Le beurre c'est meilleur!' And it's true: butter is better! I first connected with Gabriel, a long-time French chef and television personality, over butter and a shared love of keeping things simple. According to him, artisan butter is the 'crème de la crème' of French cuisine's ingredients. Gabriel grew up in the Loire Valley with homemade butter delivered by Marie, a local farmer, which his grandmother Pascaline used to prepare meals for his family of eight. As he describes, 'What a difference a knob of butter made…!' Pascaline, who cooked professionally herself, inspired Gabriel to become a chef who has gifted us with many recipes. These include this galette, which is classic Gabriel: unfussy, generous and quietly elegant, with butter right at the centre of it all.

▪ ▪ ▪ SERVES 8 ▪ ▪ ▪

200 g (7 oz) salted cultured butter, diced, at room temperature
180 g (6½ oz) caster (superfine) sugar
2 teaspoons finely grated lemon zest
4 egg yolks
160 g (5½ oz) plain (all-purpose) flour, sifted, plus extra for dusting
80 g (2¾ oz) almond meal
50 g (1¾ oz) flaked almonds
about 200 g (7 oz) blueberries, fresh or frozen
cream, to serve

Place the butter, sugar, lemon zest and 3½ of the egg yolks in the bowl of a stand mixture fitted with a blade attachment. Mix on low speed until the ingredients are combined, or mix by hand. Gradually add the flour and almond meal until they are just incorporated. Remove the dough from the bowl and shape into a ball, then flatten a little, cover with plastic wrap and refrigerate for at least 1 hour but preferably overnight.

Preheat the oven to 190°C (375°F) fan-forced and sprinkle the inside of a 24 cm (9½ in) flan tin with the flaked almonds.

Lightly beat the remaining egg yolk with 1 teaspoon of water.

Cut the dough in half. Lightly flour the dough, your hands and the rolling pin and roll each dough half out to a circle large enough to fit the tin. Place one round of dough in the tin. Top with the blueberries, leaving a 1 cm (½ in) border clear around the edge. Place the other round of dough on top and brush with the egg wash. Draw a lattice pattern on the dough using a fork.

Bake for 20 minutes, then reduce the oven to 180°C (350°F) and bake for a further 35 minutes. Leave to cool before turning out with care.

Serve with a delicious artisan cream.

Store the galette in an airtight container in the fridge for up to 3 days, or freeze for up to 3 months.

Burnt butter apple turnovers

These turnovers start with a simple butter puff pastry that's worlds away from the store-bought version. The filling is warm with apple and spices, while the pastry is buttery and light – together they make a turnover that's crisp, fragrant and not overly sweet. Cold butter is a non-negotiable for making puff pastry. If the dough softens at any point, stop and chill it – flakiness only happens when the butter stays distinct until it hits the oven.

▪ ▪ ▪ MAKES 8 ▪ ▪ ▪

1 egg, beaten with 1 tablespoon milk, for brushing
demerara sugar, for sprinkling
ice cream, to serve (optional)

BUTTER PUFF PASTRY
375 g (2½ cups) plain (all-purpose) flour, plus extra for dusting
1 teaspoon fine sea salt
300 g (11 oz) cultured butter, chilled and diced
180–200 ml (6–7 fl oz) ice-cold water

APPLE BURNT BUTTER FILLING
60 g (2 oz) unsalted cultured butter
3 apples (Granny Smith or similar), peeled, cored and diced
80 g (⅓ cup) brown sugar
1 teaspoon ground cinnamon
½ teaspoon vanilla extract
pinch of fine sea salt
1 teaspoon cornflour (corn starch; optional, if apples are very juicy)

To make the pastry, sift the flour and salt into a large bowl. Add the cold butter and toss to coat in flour, then lightly flatten some of the butter pieces with your fingertips – you want visible shards, not crumbs.

Add the ice-cold water gradually, mixing until the dough just comes together. Turn out onto a lightly floured work surface and gently press into a rough rectangle, then roll out into a 20 × 40 cm (8 × 16 in) rectangle.

Fold the top third down and the bottom third up, like a letter. Rotate 90 degrees, roll again and repeat the folds – this is one turn. Wrap in plastic wrap and refrigerate for 20–30 minutes to firm up the dough.

Repeat for another three turns, chilling between each one. After the final turn, rest the pastry in the fridge for at least 1 hour.

To make the filling, heat the butter in a pan over medium heat until it foams, turns golden brown and has a nutty aroma – watch it closely. Remove from the heat immediately. Add the apples, brown sugar, cinnamon, vanilla and salt. Return to medium heat and cook for 8–10 minutes, until the apples soften and the mixture is glossy. If very liquid, stir in the cornflour and cook for another minute.

Remove from the heat and leave to cool completely.

Roll the rested pastry on a lightly floured work surface to a thickness of 3–4 mm (⅛ in) . Cut into 8 squares, approximately 12–14 cm (5 in) each.

Spoon the cooled filling onto half of each square diagonally, leaving a 1.5 cm (½ in) border clear around the edges. Brush the edges with the egg wash and then fold in half to form triangles. Press the edges firmly to seal and, if you like, crimp with a fork. Place on a paper-lined baking tray and chill in the fridge for 20 minutes.

Meanwhile, preheat the oven to 180°C (350°F) fan-forced.

Brush the turnovers with the egg wash, sprinkle lightly with demerara sugar and score a small vent in the top of each one. Bake for 22–25 minutes, until the pastry is dark golden and crisp. Cool the turnovers slightly before serving, and, if desired, enjoy with ice cream.

If making the pastry ahead of time, wrap the uncooked pastry in plastic wrap and store in the fridge for up to 48 hours, or freeze flat and well-sealed for up to a month, thawing slowly in the fridge before use.

Store the baked turnovers at room temperature in a single layer, covered with a cloth or baking paper, to keep the pastry crisp, or store for up to 2 days in an airtight container at room temperature. Avoid refrigerating as it softens the pastry.

The turnovers can be wrapped in plastic wrap and frozen for up to 3 months – reheat from frozen in the oven until hot and crisp.

Wholegrain blood plum galettes from Urbanstead

Michael and Pippa James of Melbourne's Urbanstead bakery are deeply respected for their love of terroir and how they let ingredients lead. Those ingredients include only local butter: a decision that fundamentally shifted their process. Industrial, imported butter allows for predictability; local butter demands attention and restraint. As bakers, the pair are critical of an industry that champions convenience, but they believe a shift can happen through taste. Their dedication carries through in their recipes, which you can trust will be exceptional, like this blood plum galette. Thoughtful and quietly brilliant, it's also versatile. Try it with your favourite fruit such as figs, or go savoury with pumpkin (winter squash) and blue cheese.

▪ ▪ ▪ MAKES 6–8 ▪ ▪ ▪

1 egg, lightly beaten
100 g (3½ oz) demerara sugar

PASTRY
250 g (9 oz) wholewheat flour (or spelt flour)
100 g (3½ oz) plain (all-purpose) flour, plus extra for dusting
¾ teaspoon salt
225 g (8 oz) unsalted butter, chilled and diced
120 g (4½ oz) crème fraîche
2 teaspoons ice-cold water

FILLING
6 blood plums
90 g (3 oz) caster (superfine) sugar
½ vanilla pod, seeds scraped, or ½ teaspoon vanilla paste
½ teaspoon ground cinnamon

To make the pastry, sift the flours and salt onto a work surface, then scatter the butter on top. Use a rolling pin to roll the butter into the flour, gathering the flour in as you go. Keep rolling until the mixture has a crumbly texture, with pea-sized lumps of butter still visible.

Transfer the mixture to a large bowl and make a well in the centre. In a separate bowl, lightly whisk the crème fraîche and water together, then pour the mixture into the well. Use a spoon to gently cut the flour into the mixture until you have an even crumble texture. Using your fingertips, gently combine into a rough dough; it should have a thick, smooth and slightly sticky texture. Place on a lightly floured work surface and roll into a rectangle roughly 2 cm (¾ in) thick, with the long edge facing you.

Fold the top third down and the bottom third up, like a letter. Rotate 90 degrees and roll into a rectangle roughly 2 cm (¾ in) thick. Repeat the folds. Roll out once more into a rectangle roughly 2 cm (¾ in) thick, then wrap in plastic wrap and refrigerate for 1 hour.

Remove the pastry from the fridge and roll it out between two sheets of baking paper to a thickness of 4 mm (¼ in). Cover in plastic wrap and return to the fridge for another 30 minutes.

Line a baking tray with baking paper. Lay the pastry on a lightly floured work surface and cut out six 16 cm (6¼ in) discs; any scraps can be pushed back together, rolled again and cut into discs. Lay the discs on the baking tray, cover and refrigerate while you prepare the plums.

To prepare the filling, slice the plums in half. Leave six of the halves intact, and slice the other six into five slim wedges each. Combine the halves and wedges in a bowl. In a separate bowl, mix the sugar, vanilla and cinnamon. Add the sugar mix to the plums and toss gently with a spoon so the sugar evenly coats the fruit.

Remove the tray of pastry discs from the fridge. Place five slim wedges of plum in a circle on each disc, thin side facing out, leaving a 2 cm (¾ in) border clear around the edge. Fold the pastry border over the wedges and crimp to seal the pastry in place with the plums underneath. This will leave a gap in the centre.

Place one intact plum half cut-side-up in the gap on each disc. Cover and chill in the fridge for 30 minutes.

Meanwhile, preheat the oven to 175°C (350°F).

Remove the prepared pastry from the fridge. Brush the exposed dough with the egg wash and sprinkle with the demerara sugar. Ensure the discs are spaced evenly on the tray, with 4 cm (1½ in) between each, for an even bake.

Bake for 15 minutes and then check the plums; if they are starting to colour too quickly, loosely cover each galette with a small sheet of foil. Reduce the temperature to 165°C (330°F) and bake for another 10–15 minutes, until the pastry is golden brown. Set aside to cool for 10–15 minutes before serving.

The galettes are delicious slightly warm, but are also good at room temperature.

If making the pastry ahead of time, wrap in plastic wrap and freeze for up to 3 months. Store the baked galettes at room temperature in an airtight container for up to 3 days; the galettes are not suitable for freezing.

Chocolate buttermilk cake

Use real, full-fat cultured buttermilk for this cake – it has a rich flavour and a velvety creamy thickness that low-fat versions just can't match. The acidity in true buttermilk creates a tender crumb, supports a good rise and adds a gentle tang.

▪ ▪ ▪ SERVES 8–12 ▪ ▪ ▪

300 g (2 cups) plain (all-purpose) flour
400 g (2 cups) white sugar
60g (½ cup) unsweetened cocoa powder
2 teaspoons baking soda
1 teaspoon baking powder
½ teaspoon salt
2 large eggs
250 ml (1 cup) vegetable oil
250 ml (1 cup) cultured buttermilk, shaken
250 ml (1 cup) hot water

CHOCOLATE BUTTERMILK ICING
110 g (½ cup) salted butter
85 g (⅔ cup) unsweetened cocoa powder
375 g (3 cups) icing (confectioners') sugar, sifted
80 ml (⅓ cup) cultured buttermilk, shaken
1 teaspoon vanilla extract

Preheat the oven to 160°C (320°F) fan-forced. Grease and flour a 25 × 13 cm (10 × 5 in) loaf tin or line with baking paper.

Whisk together the flour, sugar, cocoa powder, baking soda, baking powder and salt in a large bowl and make a well in the centre. In a separate bowl, mix together the eggs, oil and buttermilk and pour into the well, whisking to combine. Add the hot water and whisk until the batter is smooth.

Pour the batter into the tin. Tap gently on the benchtop to release any air bubbles. Bake for 40–50 minutes until a skewer poked into the centre comes out clean and the cake springs back lightly when touched. Cool completely on a wire rack before turning out and icing.

To make the icing, melt the butter in a saucepan over medium–low heat. Whisk in the cocoa powder and cook over low heat for 2 minutes without letting it come to the boil. Remove from the heat and whisk in the icing sugar and buttermilk until smooth. Add the vanilla. The icing should be thick and spreadable – if you need to thin it at all, add extra buttermilk, one tablespoon at a time.

Spread the icing over the cake and leave to cool and set before serving.

Store the cake at room temperature in an airtight container for up to 3 days or freeze slices for up to 3 months. If you're serving it for an event, baking it the day before is actually ideal. Ice the cake either on the day or after it has fully cooled overnight.

Burnt butter teacake from Gippsland Jersey

Gippsland Jersey is a proudly Victorian dairy producer known for its rich golden milk from local Gippsland farms. Founded by Sallie Jones, whose passion for supporting dairy farmers and advocating for their mental health is both genuine and inspiring, the brand embodies kindness, fairness and community. Their products are primarily made using Jersey milk, so you can imagine that beautiful yellow hue in their creamy, cultured butter. If you can find it locally, it makes this recipe by Sallie even more delicious, along with their buttermilk and cream, which you can use for the whipped topping.

▪ ▪ ▪ SERVES 10 ▪ ▪ ▪

150 g (5½ oz) unsalted cultured butter, plus extra for greasing
300 g (2 cups) self-raising flour
½ teaspoon baking soda
¼ teaspoon fine sea salt
2 eggs
250 g (1¼ cups) caster (superfine) sugar
2 teaspoons vanilla extract
185 ml (¾ cup) cultured buttermilk (see Tip on page 106)
edible flowers (violas, pansies, chamomile), for decorating (optional)
icing (confectioners') sugar, for dusting
whipped cream, to serve

ROASTED STRAWBERRIES
250 g (9 oz) strawberries, hulled and halved
1 tablespoon caster (superfine) sugar
1 teaspoon balsamic vinegar

Preheat the oven to 160°C (320°F) fan-forced and line a baking tray with baking paper.

Toss the strawberries with the sugar and vinegar and spread on the tray. Roast for 15–20 minutes until syrupy and slightly caramelised. Set aside to cool.

Melt the butter in a saucepan over medium heat, swirling the pan often, until it foams and turns a golden brown and has a nutty aroma – watch it closely. Remove from the heat immediately and let it cool slightly – it needs to be still liquid but not too hot when you're mixing the batter.

Grease and line a 20 cm (8 in) round cake tin. In a bowl, whisk together the flour, baking soda and salt.

In another bowl, beat the eggs and sugar for 3–4 minutes with a wooden spoon until pale and fluffy. Slowly drizzle in the burnt butter, beating continuously, then add the vanilla. Fold in the flour alternately with the buttermilk, starting and ending with flour. Mix until just combined.

Spoon the mixture into the tin and smooth the top. Bake for 40–45 minutes or until a skewer poked into the centre comes out clean. Leave to cool in the tin for 10 minutes, then turn out onto a rack to cool completely.

Top the cake with the roasted strawberries and drizzle the syrup over the top. Decorate with edible flowers, if desired, and a dusting of icing sugar. Serve with whipped cream.

Store the teacake, untopped, in an airtight container at room temperature for up to 2 days. It it has been topped, store the cake in the fridge and bring to room temperature before serving. You can freeze slices of cake (without the strawberries) for up to 3 months; thaw at room temperature and add fresh or roasted strawberries when serving.

Vanilla cupcakes with buttercream icing

I'm from a large family of six kids, so baking was a necessity, and a cake always seemed to be in the oven. This recipe was a favourite go-to for lunch boxes or for when friends visited, but when it came to us kids making the buttercream icing, little – if any – made it onto the cakes! The cream helps soften the sweetness and makes the buttercream icing easier to spread.

▪ ▪ ▪ MAKES 12 ▪ ▪ ▪

125 g (4½ oz) salted butter, softened
150 g (¾ cup) caster (superfine) sugar
2 eggs, at room temperature
225 g (1½ cups) plain (all-purpose) flour
1½ teaspoons baking powder
pinch of salt
125 ml (½ cup) buttermilk
60 ml (¼ cup) pure/pouring cream (see page 41)
1 teaspoon vanilla extract
sprinkles, to decorate (optional)

BUTTERCREAM ICING
125 g (4½ oz) salted butter, softened
250 g (2 cups) icing (confectioners') sugar, sifted
1–2 tablespoons pure/pouring cream (see page 41)
1½ teaspoons vanilla extract

Variations

Lemon: Add the zest of 1 lemon to the cupcake batter. Replace the cream with 2 tablespoons lemon juice in the buttercream icing.

Cinnamon: Add 1 teaspoon ground cinnamon to the cupcake batter. Beat 1 teaspoon cinnamon into the buttercream icing.

Chocolate: Beat 1½ tablespoons Dutch (unsweetened) cocoa powder into the buttercream icing.

Preheat the oven to 170°C (340°F) fan-forced. Line a 12-hole muffin tin with paper cases.

Cream together the butter and sugar until pale and fluffy. Add the eggs one at a time, beating well after each addition.

In a separate bowl, whisk together the flour, baking powder and salt. Add to the batter in two batches, alternating with the buttermilk, cream and vanilla extract. Mix gently until just combined.

Spoon the mixture into the cupcake cases and bake for 18–20 minutes, until lightly golden and a skewer poked into the centre comes out clean. Leave to cool completely on a wire rack before icing.

To make the buttercream icing, whip the softened butter with electric beaters or hand beaters for 2 minutes until pale and creamy. Add the icing sugar, cream and vanilla. Whip until light and fluffy, scraping down the side of the bowl as you go.

Spread or pipe the buttercream over the cupcakes, adding sprinkles if you like.

Store the iced cupcakes in an airtight container for up to 3 days or freeze for up to 2 months. Thaw at room temperature, uncovered, before serving.

Miso butter fudge

One of my favourite TV chefs is UK-based James Martin – if the world were ever to appoint a butter ambassador, he'd surely be at the front of the queue. This recipe is inspired by one of his. When our house is craving something sweet, this is my go-to. The combination of caramel cultured butter and miso hits every note – rich, silky and just salty enough to keep you coming back for another piece... and another!

▪ ▪ ▪ MAKES 20 PIECES ▪ ▪ ▪

397 g (14 oz) tinned sweetened condensed milk
450 g (1 lb) light brown sugar
125 g (4 oz) unsalted butter
125 ml (½ cup) full-cream (whole) milk
2 tablespoons white miso paste
175 g (6 oz) white chocolate, broken into small pieces
1 teaspoon sea salt

Line a 20 cm (8 in) square baking tin with baking paper, letting it overhang the sides.

Place all the ingredients except the salt in a large non-stick saucepan. Bring to a rolling boil and cook for about 10 minutes, stirring constantly, until the temperature reaches 112–114°C (234–237°F) on a sugar thermometer.

Take off the heat, and add the white chocolate pieces. Stir the mixture gently until the chocolate is melted. Cool for 2 minutes, then whisk vigorously by hand for 1 minute before pouring the mixture into the tin. Sprinkle with the sea salt and leave to cool and firm at room temperature for 2 hours.

Cut the fudge into squares in the tin and use the paper to help you lift out the pieces.

Store the fudge in an airtight container for up to 2 weeks, in the fridge for 3–4 weeks, and up to 3 months in the freezer.

Variation

Peanut butter miso: Add 2 tablespoons of smooth peanut butter at the same time as the miso paste to add an extra layer of salty flavour.

MARISA MAURO

Ploughgate Creamery

VERMONT, USA

. . .

FROM CHEESE TO BUTTER

There are some people who don't so much *find* dairy as fall into it – heart first, sleeves rolled up, never quite able to walk away. Marisa Mauro is one of them. She was just fourteen when she stepped onto a Vermont farm and felt something click into place. On the back of her experience as a cheese-maker, making washed-rind cheese, she launched her first creamery; by 25, she'd survived a devastating fire and was certain – *absolutely* certain – that she was done with dairy forever.

But the land has its own pull. When a friend urged her to see a little hilltop farm in the Northeast Kingdom in Vermont, Marisa went reluctantly, but left knowing she'd found her home. High on that ridge, surrounded by wind, weather and stubborn beauty, she decided to start again. Cheese no longer called to her, but butter – cultured, expressive, creamy Vermont butter – did. And in 2014, Ploughgate Creamery was born.

Marisa ignored the advice of those who said a butter-only creamery would never work. Within months, demand outpaced supply. Her high-fat, slow-cultured, unapologetically rich butter won hearts in the same way dairy had once won hers. 'I love how butter makes people so happy,' she says. 'It's breakfast, lunch, dinner – a joyful staple.'

Ploughgate has quietly become one of America's most celebrated producers of cultured butter. Drawing on European tradition, Marisa cultures local cream for 24–48 hours before slow-churning it in small batches. The result is a nutty, tangy, luxuriously creamy butter, hand-wrapped in craft paper.

In 2022 she sold Ploughgate to Maplebrook Farm, a move that let the business grow while allowing her to stay on as its guiding voice. Now a mother, she still turns up for the magical moments – lifting the churn lid after the break, and inhaling that warm, tangy aroma that says the cream has become something more.

Two decades into dairy, Marisa wonders what a 'new career' might look like. But the truth is obvious: butter is in her bones. Vermont's landscape, its farmers, its food culture – they shaped her. And, through Ploughgate, she's shaping it right back, one golden batch at a time.

PLOUGHGATE CREAMERY
@ BRAGG FARM
SALTED CULTURED
BUTTER
WWW.PLOUGHGATE.COM
NET WT 8 OZ
INGREDIENTS: PASTEURIZED
CREAM, SEA SALT & CULTURES
2021 BRAGG HILL RD
FAYSTON, VERMONT

DIRECTORY OF ARTISAN BUTTER PRODUCERS

• • •

Australia, New Zealand and many other countries have seen a quiet but remarkable revival in the dairy landscape in recent decades – a return to single-origin cream, small-batch churned butter and small-scale, regionally focused production.

Across Australia, from the lush pastures of Victoria to the rolling hills of South Australia and the coastlines of Western Australia, a new wave of artisan butter-makers has emerged. These producers are guided by old-world techniques, deep respect for the land and a love of quality. Some run micro-dairies with just a handful of Jersey cows, others craft butter logs by hand to sell at local farmers' markets or to their farmstay guests, and a few are shaping the national palate through cultured, small-batch excellence. Their work is not just about flavour: it's also about sustainability, traceability, community and reclaiming butter as the rich, nourishing food it has always been meant to be.

Australia and New Zealand

LARD ASS BUTTER
Ocean Grove, Victoria
Cultured butter, flavoured butter, buttermilk, ghee, crème fraîche
Available at specialty stores, farmers' markets, online, factory direct
www.lardass.com.au

PEPE SAYA
Sydney, New South Wales
Cultured butter, ghee, buttermilk
Available at supermarkets, specialty stores, online
www.pepesaya.com.au

GIPPSLAND JERSEY
Gippsland, Victoria
Small-batch churned cultured butter, milk, cream, ghee, buttermilk, sour cream, from a Jersey-prominent herd
Available at supermarkets, specialty stores, online
www.gippslandjersey.com.au

ST DAVID DAIRY
Fitzroy, Victoria
Micro-dairy that produces cultured butter, yoghurt, buttermilk, milk, cream
Available at supermarkets, specialty stores, factory direct
www.stdavid.com.au

MADELEINE CULTURED BUTTER
Yarra Valley, Victoria
Cultured butter and flavoured butter (such as wattleseed, pepperberry and bush tomato) handmade with butter paddles
Available at specialty stores, farmers' markets
www.madeleinebutter.com.au

SCHULZ ORGANIC DAIRY
Timboon, Victoria
Organic milk, cheese and butter over 50 years and three generations
Available at specialty stores, farmers' markets
www.schulzorganicdairy.com.au

COPPERTREE FARMS
Sydney, New South Wales
White cultured butter, truffle butter
Available at supermarkets, online
www.coppertreefarms.com.au

LONG PADDOCK CHEESE
Castlemaine, Victoria
Cultured butter, buttermilk, cheese and cheese-making workshops
Available at supermarkets, specialty stores, farmers' markets
www.longpaddockcheese.com.au

DEL BOCIA BUTTER
Coburg, Victoria
Small-batch, sweet cream butter with an Italian influence, flavoured butter (including a hand-wrapped truffle butter)
Available at supermarkets, specialty stores
www.delbocia.com.au

GYMPIE FARM CHEESE & BUTTER
Gympie, Queensland
Cheese, cultured butter, buttermilk, crème fraîche
Available at specialty stores, farmers' markets
www.gympiefarmcheese.com

TOMMERUP'S DAIRY FARM
Kerry, Queensland
Cultured butter, cream, crème fraîche, yoghurt, ice cream. No waste ethos: the skimmed milk is fed to heritage pigs while calves are raised alongside the herd
Available online, factory direct
www.tommerupsdairyfarm.com.au

THE DAIRYMAN BAROSSA
Barossa, South Australia
Small-batch butter and cream from an independent anti-industrial dairy that runs just 20 Jersey cows on 80 acres
Available at specialty stores, farmers' markets
www.thedairyman.com.au

THE BUTTER PEOPLE
Perth, Western Australia
Small-batch hand-wrapped butter, flavoured butter
Available at specialty stores, farmers' markets, online
www.thebutterpeople.com.au

DEVOTED ARTISAN BUTTER
Kwinana, Western Australia
Hand-shaped butter, flavoured butter (including locally sourced flavours such as lemon myrtle, seaweed and parsley, all season dependent)
Available at specialty stores, farmers' markets, online
www.devotedartisanbutter.com

LEWIS ROAD CREAMERY
Auckland, New Zealand
High-quality sweet cream butter, flavoured butter, ice cream, milk, with a strong focus on animal welfare and environmental standards
Available at supermarkets, specialty stores
www.lewisroadcreamery.co.nz

Europe

MAISON BORDIER
France, Brittany
World-famous cultured butter, flavoured butter (from smoked salt to seaweed) using traditional methods since 1980s
Available at specialty stores, online
www.maisonbordier.com

BEILLEVAIRE FROMAGERIE & CREAMIER
Machecoul, France
Cultured butter, raw-milk butter, raw cream, flavoured butter (including seaweed, Espelette pepper and six peppers), yoghurt, cheese
Available at specialty stores, online
www.fromagerie-beillevaire.com

THE EDINBURGH BUTTER CO.
Edinburgh, Scotland
Cultured butter, buttermilk
Available at specialty stores
www.theedinburghbutterco.co.uk

AMPERSAND DAIRY
Oxfordshire, England
Cultured butter
Available at specialty stores
www.ampersanddairy.com

THE ESTATE DAIRY
Cheshire, England
Cultured butter, milk, cream, yoghurt
Available at supermarkets, specialty stores
www.theestatedairy.com

CAWS TEIFI CHEESE
Ceredigion, Wales
Cultured butter, raw-milk butter, cheese
Available at specialty stores, online, factory direct
www.teificheese.co.uk

ABERNETHY BUTTER
Craigavon, Northern Ireland
Hand-paddled, hand-wrapped butter, flavoured butter (including dulce & sea salt or chipotle chilli & smoked paprika)
Available at specialty stores, online
www.abernethybutter.com

BUNGAY BUTTER, FEN FARM DAIRY
Suffolk, England
Raw cultured butter, cheese
Available at specialty stores
www.fenfarmdairy.co.uk

ARLA UNIKA
Copenhagen, Denmark
Boutique arm of the large Arla dairy company, producing double-soured and double-kneaded cultured butter, milk, crème fraîche, kefir
Available at specialty stores, online
www.arlaunika.dk

DEN EELDER
Well, Gelderland, Netherlands
Goat milk, butter, yoghurt, buttermilk
Available at supermarkets, specialty stores
https://deneelder.nl

USA and Canada

VERMONT CREAMERY
Websterville, Vermont
European-style cultured butter, crème fraîche, since 1984
Available at supermarkets
www.vermontcreamery.com

MINERVA DAIRY
Minerva, Ohio
America's oldest family-owned creamery, founded 1894, producing high-fat, slow-churned butter, flavoured butter
Available at supermarkets, specialty stores, online
www.minervadairy.com

BANNER BUTTER
Atlanta, Georgia
Cultured butter, flavoured buttermilk
Available at supermarkets, specialty stores, online
www.bannerbutter.com

PLOUGHGATE CREAMERY
North Bennington, Vermont
Cultured butter, flavoured butter
Available at specialty stores, online
www.ploughgate.com

ANIMAL FARM CREAMERY
Shoreham, Vermont
Cultured butter, buttermilk, with a focus on animal wellbeing
Available at specialty stores, online
www.animalfarmcreamery.com

LOFTY BUTTER COMPANY
Colborne, Ontario
Handcrafted cultured butter, crème fraîche, clarified butter, flavoured butter
Available at specialty stores, farmers' markets, online
www.loftybutter.ca

ST BRIGID'S CREAMERY
Huron County, Ontario
Butter
Available at specialty stores
www.stbrigidscreamery.ca

SECRET LANDS FARM
Owen Sound, Ontario
Cultured sheep's butter, kefir
Available at specialty stores, online
www.secretlands.ca

South Africa

CREAM OF THE CROP MICRO DAIRY
Piket-Bo-Berg, South Africa
Cultured butter, buttermilk, kefir
Available at specialty stores
Instagram @creamofthecropbutter

ACKNOWLEDGEMENTS: THE STORY OF LARD ASS BUTTER

• • •

In hindsight, making butter was my destiny.

I am a dairy farmer's daughter. Antonio, my father, started a dairy farm in Glenfyne, a small hamlet in the heart of Victoria's western district with my mum Bertilla (Betty) after they migrated to Australia from Italy in the 1950s. I married a man from Jersey in the Channel Islands, where the Jersey cow originated. His name is Mike Howell, which, when you say it quickly, sounds as if you're saying 'my cow.'

See? How can you argue that it wasn't written in the stars?

During a 2014 trip to Jersey to visit Mike's family when our boys were young, we spent a week in the south of France. It was here I fell in love with French butter, thanks to a visit to La Maison du Beurre Bordier in Saint-Malo. I can clearly recall purchasing the Espelette butter and consuming it in one sitting. I didn't just marvel at my efforts to eat a packet of butter in one day, but pondered why I ate it as if it were a block of cheese. I would never eat commercial butters this way.

My butter-making journey took me down a rabbit hole where I learnt cheese-making, cultures, fermentation processes, cream, seasons, butter fat, pH readings, humidity, sanitising, agitation, moisture controls... and took a trip to Wisconsin. At the University of Wisconsin there is a department dedicated to dairy called the Center for Dairy Research, which runs the Buttermaker Apprenticeship Workshop – a week's course teaching all things butter. I registered and went. I was their only ever 'outsider' and they couldn't understand why I was there – doesn't Australia have a department for dairy production? Or a course teaching people how to make butter? They were surprised at my flat 'no.'

After 'graduating,' I came home and Lard Ass was launched. My first sale of cultured butter at the local farmers' market in Ocean Grove has a video of me dancing with the excitement of a toddler on Christmas day. I am still in touch with the lady who made that purchase!

The name Lard Ass was chosen for people to have a laugh. It's irreverent and joyful – a nudge not to take ourselves too seriously while we take the butter very seriously. Behind the joke is a lot of hard work, stainless steel, food safety plans and regular audits, sleepless nights over fermentation mishaps, power outages or broken and badly designed machinery, and a deep belief that real food made with care still matters.

This book is another part of that belief. It's my way of putting everything I've learnt – from Glenfyne to Jersey, from Saint-Malo to Wisconsin, from the farm to the churn – into your hands. If it makes you slow down long enough to really taste your butter, to ask where it came from and who made it, then Lard Ass has done its job.

Butter brought my family here. Butter keeps us together. And, with any luck, butter will carry on this story long after our particular churns have stopped.

TOP TO BOTTOM My father, Antonio, in the 1960s with the new milk cooling system he installed at the family farm in Glenfyne, Victoria, where the farm still runs today, 360 acres later; Tony and the family dog Tip with 5 out of the 12 cows my dad owned at the time. He milked them on his own until his children were old enough to help.

LARD ASS
CULTURALLY CRAFTED
Où est le beurre?
LARD ASS
SMALL BATCH
CULTURALLY
CRAFTED

THANKS...

. . .

This book would not exist without the people who have stood beside me, tasted endlessly, worked tirelessly and believed – sometimes even more than I did – that butter was worth this much care.

To my husband, Mike, my number-one fan and supporter from the very beginning of my butter-making journey, and my most trusted taste tester. Your belief never wavered, even when mine did.

To my sons – Owen, Theo and Archie – who truly live up to the 'family' in family business. Your support is unwavering and, if the business doesn't last forever, at least you will always have a deep love for good butter – which feels like a win in itself.

To my parents, who migrated from Italy to a new world and built a life from milk and mud and stubbornness.

To Adela, who puts up with my headstrong nature and whose consistent, behind-the-scenes hard work often goes unnoticed simply because the business runs as it should. That is no small achievement.

To my brothers, Julian and Louie, and their families – dairy is in the blood, and I am proud of you for carrying that forward. And to my sister, Elena, for always stepping in with big-sister wisdom exactly when it was needed.

With thanks and deep appreciation to Carole Willman. Cheese brought us together, but butter is what made us lifelong friends. You have been a huge influence on my journey, and I will never forget your unwavering support and kindness throughout it.

To Bob – what you thought was done for fun became something much more.

To my team at Lard Ass Butter – you guys love butter as much as me and this is what keeps the churns churning.

To the butter-makers, chefs and bakers who contributed to this book by sharing their stories and recipes. Each story is unique, each personality behind the craft a treasure. May we see many more books about butter in the years to come.

To Megan and Smith Street Books for believing Australia needs a butter book – thank you for reaching out of the blue and asking me to write a book about butter. It was an *omg!* moment and, somehow, we did it. Your email will forever be framed on my wall. To Avery and Jane, thank you for your guidance, patience and support, and for making this such a genuinely wonderful experience. You've made me want to embark on another book adventure – which says everything.

This book is also a thank you to the cows, and to the farmers who get up in the dark and the cold. Without their care, labour and commitment, none of what we make – or enjoy – would be possible.

Finally, a butter-loving thank you to our customers for choosing our butter or any other artisan butter. This book is written for you. Your support sustains this work, and your choice to buy thoughtfully and eat well is what allows small-scale butter-making to endure.

FURTHER READING

. . .

Butter: A Rich History by Elaine Khosrova

The Dairy Book of Home Cookery by Sonia Allison

Home Cheese Making by Ricki Carroll

The Art of Fermentation by Sandor Katz

The Whole Beast: Nose to Tail Eating by Fergus Henderson

Spoiled: The Myth of Milk as a Superfood by Anne Mendelson

Butter Passion by Jean-Yves Bordier

Butter: A Celebration by Olivia Potts

Milk Made: A Book about Cheese by Nick Haddow

Lincoln's Place: The Story of an Australian Pioneer Farm by Colin Thiele and Robert Ingpen

Milk! A 10,000-Year Food Fracas by Mark Kurlansky

Milk: A Local and Global History by Deborah Valenze

The Secret Life of Cows by Rosamund Young

Buttermilk by Diane St Clair

Bread & Butter: History, Culture, Recipes by Richard Snapes, Grant Harrington and Eve Hemmingway

Better Butter by Robert Bradley (Center for Dairy Research, University of Wisconsin)

Butter through the Ages at webexhibits.org

INDEX

. . .

Smith Street Books

Published in 2026 by Smith Street Books
Naarm (Melbourne) | Australia
smithstreetbooks.com

Distributed outside of ANZ, North & Latin America by Thames & Hudson Ltd.,
6–24 Britannia Street, London, WC1X 9JD
thamesandhudson.com

EU Authorised Representative:
Interart S.A.R.L. 19 rue Charles Auray,
93500 Pantin, Paris, France
productsafety@thameshudson.co.uk;
www.interart.fr

ISBN: 978-1-9235-0346-5

Smith Street Books respectfully acknowledges the Wurundjeri People of the Kulin Nation, who are the Traditional Owners of the land on which we work, and we pay our respects to their Elders past and present.

Publisher: Megan Cuthbert
Project editor: Avery Hayes
Editor: Jane Price
Food photographer: Daniel Herrmann-Zoll
Food stylist: Lee Blaylock
Food prep: Caroline Griffiths and Claire Pietersen
Farm photographer: Nish Paranavitana
Design concept: Claire Rochford
Design layout and prepress: Megan Ellis
Proofreader: Kirsty van der Veer
Indexer: Max McMaster
Production manager: Aisling Coughlan

Printed & bound in China by
C&C Offset Printing Co., Ltd.

Book 486
10 9 8 7 6 5 4 3 2 1

FSC www.fsc.org MIX Paper | Supporting responsible forestry FSC® C008047